The Collective Mind

Harnessing Group Power

By
Mason D. Abbott

The Collective Mind

Harnessing Group Power

Table of Contents

Introduction

In a world increasingly driven by the power of collective action, understanding how groups function is more essential than ever. Groups are woven into the fabric of our daily lives—whether at work, in community settings, or even online. Each group interaction shares a fundamental premise: the whole is greater than the sum of its parts. Yet, achieving this synergy requires more than just bringing people together; it demands a deep understanding of group dynamics, psychology, decision-making, and communication. This book is an exploration of these dynamics, offering insights and strategies to unlock the full potential of working together.

From business leaders striving for efficiency to social scientists seeking to decode human behavior, the allure of understanding group dynamics spans numerous fields. For managers and team coordinators, mastering these principles can result in more innovative solutions and productive outcomes. For individuals, an understanding of group psychology can enhance personal interactions, build trust, and navigate conflicts more effectively.

At its core, this guide is about more than just academic theory; it's about practical applications that resonate in everyday scenarios. Group dynamics don't just influence business meetings—they manifest in classrooms, social movements, neighborhoods, and even virtual spaces. Each chapter will delve into different aspects of group behavior, offering tools to harness collective strengths and mitigate drawbacks.

The psychology of group behavior forms the backbone of this understanding. Social identity, peer influence, and group decision-making processes significantly impact individual decisions and feelings. By shedding light on these psychological underpinnings, this book aims to provide readers with insights to foster positive interactions in any group setting.

Leadership is another critical component, deeply intertwined with group dynamics. Effective leaders not only influence outcomes but also shape group culture and dynamics. The exploration of various leadership styles and their impacts will help outline how intentional leadership can guide groups toward achieving common goals while respecting individuality.

Communication within groups can either be a strength or a stumbling block, depending on how it's managed. Effective communication strategies are central to building trust and ensuring cohesion, especially in diverse teams. Understanding and overcoming communication barriers is crucial for maintaining effective interaction in various settings, including remote work environments—a growing reality in today's technology-driven world.

Diversity is often touted as a strength within groups, but it requires careful management to be truly beneficial. By embracing varied perspectives, teams can foster innovation and creativity, moving beyond conventional solutions and thinking. However, diversity also brings challenges that, if ignored, can lead to misunderstandings and conflicts.

Conflicts are inevitable in any group, but they don't have to be destructive. This book will offer techniques for identifying and managing conflicts effectively, transforming potential disruptions into opportunities for growth. It's through these processes that groups can emerge stronger and more unified.

Motivation and performance are intertwined within the fabric of group dynamics. Factors influencing group motivation are complex and multifaceted, involving both individual and collective elements. Through an understanding of these factors, group leaders and members can devise strategies to boost performance and achieve shared objectives.

Incorporating emotional intelligence is paramount in understanding group dynamics. The emotional undercurrents within a group can significantly influence interactions and outcomes. This exploration will highlight how managing emotions can lead to healthier, more productive environments.

As the nature of teams and collaboration evolves, so too do the challenges and opportunities presented by technology. The rise of virtual teams and digital tools has redefined traditional boundaries, necessitating new strategies for effective remote collaboration and overcoming technological hurdles.

Avoiding common pitfalls like groupthink is essential for maintaining creative and effective group interactions. By understanding its signs and impacts, groups can take proactive steps to encourage open dialogue and prevent the stifling of innovation.

The book also addresses ethical considerations, recognizing the importance of maintaining integrity within group interactions. Developing ethical guidelines can ensure that a team's achievements are both effective and morally sound.

Finally, no discussion of group dynamics would be complete without examining outcomes. Measuring effectiveness and learning from various metrics can guide continuous improvement and team development, ensuring that groups remain adaptable and forward-thinking in an ever-changing landscape.

This comprehensive exploration isn't just a guide for understanding group dynamics—it's a tool for mastering them. By delving into various facets of collective behavior, individuals and leaders alike can harness this understanding to foster personal and professional growth, capitalizing on the long-term benefits of effective group interactions. Together, we'll navigate the complexities of working with others, ensuring that every interaction moves toward greater cooperation, understanding, and success.

Chapter 1:
Understanding Group Dynamics

At the heart of any successful team or collective endeavor lies a fundamental understanding of group dynamics. It's more than just a collection of individuals; it's an intricate dance of personalities, roles, and shared goals. Delving into the nature of groups reveals a social microcosm where diverse elements merge and, at times, clash, creating a unique environment that influences behavior and outcomes. Key elements of group interaction include communication, cohesion, and conflict—they shape the pathways through which groups evolve and transform. By grasping these dynamics, leaders and members alike can unlock the potential to harness collective energy effectively, propelling both personal growth and societal advancement. The strength of a group lies not only in its numbers but in its ability to function harmoniously, adapting to challenges with resilience and innovation. Understanding these nuances gives one the tools not just to participate in groups but to lead them toward meaningful achievements.

The Nature of Groups

Understanding the nature of groups requires delving into the essence of what makes them tick. Groups, whether they're business teams, social clubs, or volunteer organizations, are more than just a collection of individuals. They are dynamic entities with complex interactions that influence members' behaviors, decisions, and emotions. This dance between individuality and collective identity is at the heart of group dynamics and forms the foundation for understanding how groups function.

At the most basic level, a group is defined by a shared purpose or goal that brings individuals together. This purpose-oriented approach lays the groundwork for collaboration. It's the glue that keeps members aligned despite differences that may exist among them. Within the framework of a group, individuals find a collective identity, which can lead to enhanced motivation and commitment toward shared objectives. In essence, when people come together with a common cause, they often find the drive to overcome obstacles that they might not tackle alone.

Yet, groups are not merely about shared goals. They also manifest in the relationships and roles that form among members. Each person enters a group with their unique perspectives and skills. These differences can enrich the group's functioning if harnessed correctly, leading to innovative ideas and solutions. However, understanding and integrating these diverse perspectives is often challenging. Group members must navigate through various interpersonal dynamics, such as power hierarchies, informal roles, and personal biases, which can either bolster or hinder their effectiveness.

Furthermore, the size of a group can significantly impact its dynamics. Smaller groups tend to foster closer relationships and create a stronger sense of accountability among members. Communication is often more direct and effective, reducing the risk of misunderstanding and conflict. However, smaller groups might struggle with a limited range of skills and viewpoints. In contrast, larger groups bring diverse skills and ideas but might face challenges in coordination and maintaining cohesion. Thus, achieving an optimal group size is crucial to balancing these dynamics effectively. Each size carries its unique advantages and challenges, and understanding when and how to utilize them is vital.

The cohesion of a group heavily depends on the development of trust among its members. Trust acts as a lubricant for interpersonal interactions, allowing individuals to take risks and share ideas without fear of judgment or rejection. When trust is present, groups can engage in constructive debate, problem-solving, and decision-making. On the flip side, a lack of trust leads to fear, confusion, and disengagement, stalling progress. Building and maintaining trust is a continuous process that requires intentional effort and transparency from all members.

The roles individuals assume within groups often emerge naturally and may shift based on the group's needs. These roles can be formal, such as assigned leadership positions, or informal, like becoming the group's moral compass or conflict mediator. Recognizing these roles is essential for smooth functioning and for leveraging the strengths that each member brings. However, rigidly defined roles can inhibit creativity and reduce flexibility, so it's important that groups remain adaptable, evolving in response to changing circumstances.

Moreover, the stage of development a group is in can significantly influence its dynamic nature. Groups often evolve through stages such as forming, storming, norming, performing, and, sometimes, adjourning. Each stage presents its own set of challenges and opportunities. For instance, the "storming" phase might be stressful as members vie for roles or encounter conflicts due to differences in opinions or working styles. However, successfully navigating this stage often leads to norming, where clearer roles and stronger norms for behavior emerge, eventually leading to the 'performing' phase where the group operates at its most effective.

In groups, culture also plays a pivotal role, subtly yet powerfully influencing how members interact. Cultural backgrounds and shared experiences shape expectations, norms, and communication styles within a group. Leveraging these differences can enrich the group's output, while also presenting challenges if not acknowledged and embraced. Groups need to cultivate an environment of inclusivity where all cultural perspectives are valued and integrated into their functioning.

The interplay between individual identity and collective identity within groups adds another layer of complexity. Members bring personal goals that can sometimes diverge from the group's overarching purpose. Balancing personal and group goals calls for establishing a tolerant and open atmosphere, encouraging dialogue that aligns individual aspirations with the collective mission. This harmony not only benefits the group but also nurtures individual growth and satisfaction. When people feel their personal contributions are recognized and valued, their investment in the group's success deepens, yielding benefits on both fronts.

Finally, the physical and virtual environments in which groups operate can greatly impact their dynamics. An environment conducive to collaboration can stimulate engagement and creativity, while a restrictive one might stifle interaction. Virtual groups face additional hurdles such as technological barriers and the absence of non-verbal cues, making it essential to adapt strategies to maintain effective communication and connection. Embracing tools that support virtual interactions and ensuring inclusivity in digital spaces can mitigate potential downsides.

In sum, the nature of groups is a multifaceted subject that encompasses various elements including shared goals, trust, roles, cultural influences, and environments. By understanding these aspects, individuals and leaders can better navigate the complexities of group dynamics. This understanding is key to fostering environments where groups can thrive, reach their potential, and achieve common objectives through cohesive, collaborative efforts. As you continue to explore further into group dynamics, consider how each element plays a crucial part in the collective mosaic, turning simple interactions into profound, productive engagements.

Key Elements of Group Interaction

Understanding group dynamics necessitates a deep dive into the key elements that shape group interactions. These elements form the backbone of how groups function and interact, influencing outcomes in both perceptible and subtle ways. Within any group, whether it's a corporate team, a social club, or a study group, the fundamental dynamics are often dictated by factors such as group structure, communication patterns, and individual roles. Recognizing these elements offers valuable insight into how groups collaborate effectively or falter in their endeavors.

One of the primary elements of group interaction is the structure of the group itself. This refers to the way in which a group is organized and how roles are distributed among its members. A well-structured group has clarity in its hierarchy, if one exists, as well as in the roles each member plays, allowing for smoother interactions and more effective task execution. Structure can dictate communication flow, decision-making opportunities, and ultimately, group efficiency. However, it's important to note that not all groups benefit from rigid structures; some thrive on fluidity and are most successful when roles are flexible, allowing creativity to flourish.

Group norms are another critical element, serving as the shared guidelines or rules that shape interactions within the group. These norms help in creating an acceptable behavioral standard and are often unwritten yet understood implicitly by the members. A group with strong, positive norms can create an environment that nurtures trust and collaboration, encouraging members to contribute their best efforts. In contrast, negative norms can stifle interaction, leading to conflicts and disengagement.

The influence of individual roles within a group cannot be overstated. Every group member brings their unique strengths and perspectives, contributing to the collective success. Identifying the role that best suits each individual enhances group dynamics as members can leverage their skills to provide maximum value. An understanding of these roles helps prevent role ambiguity and role conflict, which can disrupt group harmony and performance. It fosters an environment where each member understands their contributions, leading to cohesive teamwork.

Furthermore, the balance between task-oriented and relationship-oriented interactions is pivotal in group dynamic success. Task-oriented interactions focus on the achievement of group objectives and completion of tasks, ensuring the group accomplishes its goals efficiently. Meanwhile, relationship-oriented interactions emphasize the well-being and development of group members, fostering a supportive and emotionally nurturing environment. A group that excels in balancing these interactions tends to achieve its objectives while maintaining strong interpersonal relationships among its members.

Communication patterns within a group are the lifeline of interactions. Effective communication can break down barriers, bridge gaps, and facilitate the exchange of innovative ideas. Groups that prioritize open communication practices enable members to express their thoughts candidly, fostering an environment of continuous feedback and learning. Miscommunications, on the other hand, can breed misunderstandings and disengagement; thus, honing communication skills is critical to enhancing group interactions and preventing friction.

Decision-making processes are also a cornerstone of group interaction. The approach taken to reach decisions can significantly affect group dynamics and outcomes. Whether a group operates through consensus, democratic voting, or authoritative decision-making, understanding the chosen method's implications is crucial. Each approach has its strengths and challenges, and selecting the most suitable one depends on the group's objectives, structure, and the nature of the decision at hand.

The impact of psychological safety on group interactions cannot be overlooked. When members feel safe to express themselves without fear of retribution or ridicule, the group thrives on creativity and collective problem-solving. Psychological safety is cultivated through trust-building exercises and respectful communication, ensuring that all voices are heard and valued. This feeling of safety allows group members to take interpersonal risks, leading to innovative solutions and increased group cohesion.

An often underestimated aspect of group interaction is the diversity of the group. Diversity encompasses a variety of dimensions, including cultural backgrounds, skill sets, and personal experiences. When harnessed effectively, diversity can enrich group interactions by introducing a broad spectrum of perspectives, leading to enhanced problem-solving capabilities and creativity. However, leveraging diversity requires a conscious effort to foster an inclusive environment where different perspectives are genuinely valued and encouraged.

The dynamics of power and influence also significantly shape group interactions. Power within a group may be derived from a variety of sources, including positional authority, expertise, or interpersonal connections. Understanding how power operates allows groups to manage influence equitably, ensuring that decisions are made based on merit rather than dominance. Effective group interactions often balance authority with inclusivity, promoting a culture where influence is earned through contribution and value.

Within these complex webs of interaction, conflict is inevitable. While conflict is often seen negatively, it can be a catalyst for growth and innovation if managed constructively. Groups that openly address conflicts and view them as opportunities for learning and development tend to emerge stronger and more cohesive. By establishing clear conflict resolution mechanisms, groups can navigate disagreements with respect and understanding, turning potential disruptions into avenues for progress.

Emotion management within groups plays a significant role in interaction dynamics. Emotions can be contagious, and the mood of group members can affect the overall group atmosphere. Being attuned to emotional undercurrents and addressing negative emotions effectively can boost morale and productivity. Groups that acknowledge and harness emotions constructively enhance member satisfaction and strengthen collective resilience.

Finally, feedback mechanisms are vital for refining group interactions continuously. Constructive feedback loops allow members to reflect on their contributions and group processes, identify areas of improvement, and celebrate successes. Continual feedback fosters a culture of growth and adaptability, enabling groups to respond proactively to challenges and seize opportunities for advancement.

In essence, the key elements of group interaction are interconnected threads that, when addressed with intention and awareness, create strong and resilient group dynamics. By understanding and integrating these elements, groups can not only maximize their performance but also enrich the experiences of each member, elevating their collective capacity to achieve great things together.

Chapter 2:
The Psychology of Group Behavior

Group behavior is a fascinating dance of influences and identities that shapes our interactions and transforms the collective experience. Each individual, though unique, finds themselves drifting towards a shared identity within a group, often swayed by the subtle forces of social dynamics. In groups, the line between personal and collective identity blurs, leading individuals to adopt behaviors they might not exhibit alone. Understanding this psychology reveals that groups can amplify individual strengths or exacerbate weaknesses, highlighting the critical role of social identity. As members align with group norms and values, their behaviors and decisions often reflect the collective will—sometimes at the cost of personal judgment. Recognizing these influences empowers leaders and participants alike to create environments that foster positive collaboration and harness the constructive potential within groups. By comprehending how individual behavior interplays with group dynamics, we can unlock pathways to effective teamwork and enriched communal experiences, ultimately steering the group towards shared success and innovation.

How Groups Influence Individuals

Groups have a profound ability to shape the behaviors, thoughts, and emotions of their individual members. This influence can be both explicit, as seen in clear social norms, and implicit, subtly guiding individual actions through unspoken cultural cues. The impact groups hold over individuals is rooted in our innate social nature and the psychological processes that govern group dynamics. Individuals often find themselves navigating their identities, motivations, and even decision-making processes within the context of a group setting.

One of the core ways that groups influence individuals is through the establishment of social norms. These norms dictate what is deemed acceptable or unacceptable within the group and serve as a powerful motivator for conformity. Social norms can foster a sense of belonging and community among group members, which in turn can enhance cooperation and facilitate harmonious interactions. When members adhere to these social norms, they contribute to the cohesion of the group, often prioritizing group harmony over individual desires.

Social identity theory provides another lens through which to understand the group's impact on the individual. The theory suggests that people derive a significant part of their self-concept from the social groups they belong to. This identification with the group can boost self-esteem and give individuals a sense of pride and belonging. However, it can also lead to in-group favoritism and out-group discrimination, demonstrating the implicit power of group identity to influence perceptions and behaviors.

The need for acceptance and approval within a group setting often leads individuals to conform to group standards and expectations, sometimes even against their own beliefs or values. This conformity can be conscious or subconscious and can manifest through subtle peer pressure or the overt reinforcement of group norms. In some cases, individuals might find themselves agreeing with group decisions that contradict their personal opinions, a phenomenon that underscores the impact of groupthink on individual cognition.

Moreover, social comparison within groups can significantly affect individual behavior. Members may constantly gauge their own abilities and opinions against those of their peers, which can either motivate self-improvement or lead to feelings of inadequacy. In competitive environments, this comparison might spur members to perform better, while in supportive groups, it can enhance learning and personal growth.

A key factor in understanding group influence is the notion of social facilitation, where the presence of others can increase individual performance on simple or well-rehearsed tasks. Conversely, complex or unfamiliar tasks may see decreased performance due to increased anxiety or self-awareness when being observed by the group. This highlights how the mere physiological arousal prompted by a group setting can impact productivity and outcomes.

Leaning into the motivational aspects of group influence, individuals can find empowerment through collective efforts. Participation in a group often brings about a shared sense of purpose, sparking motivation and inspiring members to push beyond personal limitations. Through collaborative endeavors, group synergy emerges, where the combined effort results in greater achievement than what individuals might accomplish alone.

However, the darker side of group influence cannot be ignored. Groups can propagate negative behaviors and attitudes, such as polarizing opinions or fostering exclusionary practices. Individuals might find their personal values compromised when submerged in cultures of group pressure that reward conformity at the stake of diversity of thought. It is in these contexts that ethical leadership becomes paramount to steward group influence positively.

Individuals also experience indirect influences through observational learning within group environments. By watching the successes and failures of peers, members can adopt new strategies and behaviors that align with perceived desirable outcomes. This vicarious experience enriches the individual's learning curve and promotes adaptation to group demands without direct trial and error.

The unique interplay of group membership dynamics, such as roles, status, and hierarchies, profoundly shapes individual behavior and perception. High-status members might have more liberty and leeway in behavior, whereas lower-status individuals often exert more energy navigating group politics to gain acceptance or upward mobility. The balance of these roles and their impact on individual autonomy is a delicate dance that requires both self-awareness and strategic social maneuvering.

In summary, groups wield significant influence over individuals by setting social norms, shaping identities, and facilitating behavior through various psychological mechanisms. This influence can foster personal growth and inspire greater achievements when managed constructively. However, it also risks precipitating negative outcomes if group dynamics promote rigidity, conformity, or view diversity with skepticism. Understanding these dynamics and the intricate relationship between group influence and individual behavior provides a pathway to leveraging group psychology for positive, transformative outcomes. Being aware of these influences equips leaders and members alike to shape group environments that harness collective potential while respecting individual integrity.

The Role of Social Identity

Stepping into the world of social identity reveals a profound understanding of group behavior. At its core, social identity is the part of an individual's self-concept that stems from their membership in a social group. It's not merely about belonging to a group but involves the emotional significance attached to that membership. This connection isn't just superficial—it's deeply embedded in one's self-understanding and behavior. Social identity guides how we interact within groups as well as our perceptions of in-group and out-group members.

Understanding how social identity shapes behavior involves examining why people feel drawn to certain groups in the first place. People naturally gravitate toward groups that reflect their values, beliefs, and experiences. For instance, a person passionate about environmental conservation might join a group dedicated to environmental activism. This belongingness not only bolsters self-esteem but also strengthens collective goals, driving individuals toward greater cooperation and group cohesion. Such identification can lead to amplified efforts and enthusiasm, particularly when group goals align closely with personal values.

However, social identity isn't just a tool for unity—it can also be a source of division. The concepts of "us" versus "them" often arise, as individuals become highly attuned to distinctions between their group and others. This categorization can lead to stereotyping, bias, and even discrimination, influencing how individuals within a group view outsiders. Boundaries are drawn, sometimes quite rigidly, affecting how collective resources are utilized or how decisions are made. Overcoming these divides requires conscious effort and awareness of the biases that stem from social identity.

Another fascinating aspect of social identity is its influence on behavior and attitudes even when individuals are not consciously aware of it. Social categorization activates associated norms and stereotypes, which can implicitly guide decisions and interactions. This might manifest as adopting group norms regarding dress codes, language, or even decision-making styles. Often, the influence is automatic; people might not realize they're conforming until viewed in retrospect. Such unconscious adherence to group norms ensures stability and predictability within the group, aiding in seamless interactions and a unified approach toward common goals.

Leadership plays a pivotal role in shaping and directing social identities within a group. Effective leaders can harness the power of social identity to inspire commitment and drive. When leaders articulate a clear and cohesive group identity, they encourage members to see beyond personal preferences and embrace shared objectives. This empowerment through social identity can galvanize efforts, promoting resilience and adaptability, especially in challenging situations. Conversely, leaders who fail to acknowledge or respect the social identities within their groups may find it challenging to foster long-term cohesion and loyalty.

Social identity also operates as a reservoir of motivation. When individuals strongly identify with a group, they often display heightened levels of motivation to contribute to group success. This can manifest in a variety of ways, from increased participation in meetings to willingness to undertake additional responsibilities without direct rewards. The motivation derived from a strong group identity is not solely about individual achievement; rather, it's about enhancing the group's status, achievements, and overall well-being.

Within the realm of social identity, intersecting identities add layers of complexity. Individuals simultaneously belong to multiple groups—be it cultural, professional, or interest-based—each contributing to a multifaceted social identity. Navigating these identities requires a dynamic understanding of conflicts and synergies. A person might find themselves at an intersection that demands juggling different identities depending on context. This fluidity necessitates skills in mediating conflicts and merging various identity aspects to harmonize group interactions.

Interactions among groups, when guided by social identity awareness, can lead to collaboration and mutual learning. Group members armed with a strong sense of identity tend to engage more meaningfully in dialogues, valuing diverse perspectives. This openness can foster innovation and creativity, which are crucial in solving complex problems and facing new challenges. By understanding and respecting multiple identities, groups can leverage this diversity to enhance problem-solving and decision-making capabilities.

Ultimately, the understanding and navigation of social identity within groups is a crucial skill for anyone looking to harness the full potential of collective behavior. It offers insights into constructing cohesive teams that are not only high-performing but also inclusive and considerate of diverse perspectives. By recognizing and actively shaping social identities, leaders and group members alike can build environments where every member's identity is valued, leading to a more harmonious and effective group dynamic.

As we explore further into the psychology of group behavior, the role of social identity stands as a pillar of understanding. Its dynamics offer clues into the intricacies of human behavior, shining a spotlight on how individuals can come together to achieve collective success. Understanding social identity doesn't just enhance theoretical knowledge—it's a transformative tool for reshaping groups, fostering cooperation, and nurturing environments that thrive on collaboration.

Chapter 3:
Decision-Making in Groups

In the realm of group dynamics, decision-making stands as both an art and a science. Groups hold the potential to harness diverse perspectives, fostering creativity and innovation that outstrip individual capabilities. Yet, these benefits come with their own set of challenges. Diverse opinions can lead to richer solutions but also invite conflict and indecision. The balance between these forces requires a deep understanding of how individuals interact within groups. Effective decision-making in a group hinges on creating an environment where members feel valued and free to share their ideas. This involves leveraging structured techniques that facilitate consensus while respecting individual insights. By doing so, groups can unlock their collective potential, moving toward goals with clarity and shared commitment. Ultimately, mastering group decision-making not only leads to more effective solutions but also cultivates an atmosphere of mutual trust and inspiration.

The Pros and Cons of Group Decisions

When groups come together to make decisions, the dynamics at play can lead to powerful outcomes or significant setbacks. At the heart of this dynamic lies a complex interplay of shared knowledge, diverse perspectives, and collective reasoning, all of which can transform the way decisions are formulated and executed. Understanding the balance of pros and cons is crucial for anyone aiming to harness the full potential of group decision-making in any setting.

One of the most compelling advantages of group decision-making is the pooling of diverse perspectives. When individuals from a variety of backgrounds and with different experiences come together, they bring unique insights and ideas. This diversity of thought tends to lead to more comprehensive problem-solving since it allows for a broader understanding of the issue at hand and more innovative solutions. This advantage is particularly beneficial in complex situations where a multifaceted approach is needed.

Moreover, group decisions can enhance objectives' legitimacy and acceptance. Individuals are more likely to support decisions when they feel they've been part of the process. This participation creates a sense of ownership and accountability for the outcome, which can lead to greater commitment from team members to implement the decision effectively. This buy-in is invaluable in organizational settings, where collective effort is often required to drive projects forward.

Despite these advantages, group decision-making also has its downsides. A well-documented phenomenon is the tendency towards groupthink, where the desire for harmony or conformity in the group leads to irrational or dysfunctional decision-making outcomes. When groupthink takes over, critical thinking is stifled, and dissenting opinions are suppressed, often leading to suboptimal decisions. This phenomenon underscores the importance of fostering an environment where all group members feel comfortable voicing different opinions.

Another potential drawback is decision paralysis. With more people involved, the decision-making process can become cumbersome, sometimes leading to delays as the group struggles to reach a consensus. This issue is exacerbated when the group lacks a clear leader or decision-making framework, allowing discussions to drift without resolution. To mitigate this, it's crucial for groups to set clear agendas and time limits for decision-making processes, ensuring they stay focused and productive.

Effective communication is essential in ensuring that the benefits of group decisions outweigh the drawbacks. Good communication allows for the free exchange of ideas and helps bridge the gap between different perspectives. It also involves active listening, where group members genuinely consider others' viewpoints, fostering a collaborative spirit that can drive innovative solutions. Thus, honing communication skills within the group can significantly enhance the quality of decisions made.

In efforts to improve group decisions, certain techniques can be employed. For instance, structured decision-making frameworks like the Delphi method or the nominal group technique can help guide discussions and ensure that diverse perspectives are considered methodically. Brainstorming sessions can be structured to encourage creative thinking while minimizing the risk of groupthink by initially separating idea generation from evaluation phases.

The size of the group can also impact decision quality. While larger groups may offer more perspectives, they can also become unwieldy, leading to inefficiencies and diluted accountability. Smaller groups may foster better engagement and quicker consensus, but they might lack the diversity of thought that larger groups provide. Thus, finding a balance in group size is key, depending on the decision's complexity and nature.

The role of leadership cannot be overstated. A strong leader who creates an inclusive environment, encourages diverse viewpoints, and facilitates consensus can greatly enhance the decision-making process. However, leaders must also be careful not to dominate discussions or sway decisions unduly, as this can undermine the group's collective input and lead to biased outcomes.

Ultimately, the effectiveness of group decision-making rests on a nuanced understanding of its potential benefits and pitfalls. By leveraging diverse perspectives and ensuring active participation and clear communication, groups can make more informed decisions. However, awareness and strategies must be in place to mitigate risks like groupthink and decision paralysis. As such, cultivating a culture of openness and critical evaluation within groups is paramount to truly mastering the art of collective decision-making.

Techniques for Improving Group Decision-Making

In the realm of group dynamics, decision-making stands as one of the most critical yet complex processes. Groups often have the potential to harness collective intelligence and diverse perspectives, which can lead to superior outcomes compared to individual decisions. However, the same diversity and multitude of viewpoints can also result in decision paralysis or poor outcomes if not managed effectively. Understanding and implementing techniques to enhance group decision-making can significantly optimize the decision quality and foster a more collaborative environment.

One effective technique is to establish clear decision-making processes. Groups often struggle due to ambiguous or undefined processes, which can lead to confusion and conflict. By creating a structured framework, such as defined roles, decision rules, and clear timelines, groups can navigate their discussions more effectively. This structure helps ensure that all opinions are heard and considered, and it sets the stage for a balanced deliberation. Such frameworks could include assigning specific roles like a facilitator, who guides the discussion, or a devil's advocate, who challenges predominant views to ensure robust debate.

Another technique crucial for improving group decision-making is fostering a culture of psychological safety. When individuals feel safe to express their opinions, regardless of how they might differ from the majority, the group benefits from a richer discussion. Psychological safety encourages openness, reduces fear of judgment, and allows for constructive conflict. Leaders and group members can promote this environment by valuing contributions, acknowledging mistakes as learning opportunities, and actively soliciting diverse viewpoints.

Utilizing decision-making models, such as the Delphi Method, can also enhance the quality of decisions. This method involves gathering feedback from a panel of experts through several rounds of questioning, with the aim of reaching a consensus. It is particularly effective for complex decisions where expert insight is invaluable. By synthesizing diverse expert opinions and leveraging anonymity, the Delphi Method minimizes the influence of dominant personalities and biases that might skew collective judgment.

Moreover, groups can adopt the Nominal Group Technique (NGT) to better facilitate decision-making. The NGT involves generating ideas silently and independently before discussing them as a group. This approach prevents early filtering of ideas, allows for equal participation, and reduces the risk of groupthink. Once all ideas are shared, the group discusses and ranks them, ensuring a democratic selection process and strengthening the collective decision's legitimacy.

Integrating data-driven decision-making is yet another powerful approach. By leveraging data analytics and leveraging tools like SWOT analysis (Strengths, Weaknesses, Opportunities, Threats), groups can base their decisions on empirical evidence rather than solely on intuition or anecdotal evidence. Data can also serve as a neutral ground during debates, helping to bridge conflicting opinions by highlighting objective insights.

Effective communication is vital for improving decision-making within groups. Clear, open, and honest communication supports the exchange of ideas and reduces misunderstandings. Utilizing visual aids, like diagrams and charts, can help in presenting data and concepts clearly and engagingly. Active listening, where group members genuinely invest in understanding each other's perspectives, goes hand in hand with effective communication and leads to more informed decision outcomes.

Training in decision-making skills and group dynamics can further enhance any group's effectiveness. Providing training opportunities helps members develop valuable skills such as critical thinking, problem-solving, and negotiation. Through workshops and role-playing exercises, group members can practice decision-making in a risk-free environment, learning how to adhere to structured processes and communicate effectively.

Encouraging diverse perspectives within the group is essential for robust decision-making. Diversity in thought can be achieved by including individuals from different backgrounds, experiences, and expertise areas. Such diversity not only enriches the pool of ideas but also can act as a safeguard against groupthink, which is the tendency for homogeneous groups to converge quickly on a suboptimal solution without adequate discussion.

Reflective practices can also enhance group decision-making. After a decision has been made, it can be beneficial for groups to engage in reflection sessions where they analyze the decision-making process itself. This exercise allows groups to identify what worked well and areas for improvement, ensuring that the group continuously evolves and refines its approach to decision-making.

Finally, patience and flexibility should not be underestimated in their importance. Decision-making in a group can be time-consuming and often requires the flexibility to adapt processes as the group learns what works best for them. Patience allows for thoughtful deliberation and minimizes impulsive decisions, thereby enhancing the overall quality of the outcomes.

By implementing these techniques, groups can significantly improve their decision-making processes. The result isn't just better decisions but a more cohesive and effective team, ready to tackle complex challenges with confidence. As groups embrace these strategies, they unlock the full potential of collective wisdom, navigate complexity with greater ease, and make impactful decisions that benefit both their team and their larger organizational objectives.

Chapter 4:
Leadership and Group Influence

Leadership plays a pivotal role in shaping the dynamics and effectiveness of a group. When we talk about influential leaders, we're really examining how different styles can drive a group toward success or derail its efforts. Charismatic leaders often inspire by creating a compelling vision, while transactional leaders focus on structure and rewards. Both styles have their place, depending on the group's needs. But it's more than just choosing a leadership style; it's about understanding how leaders can adapt their approaches to fit the unique context of each group. A leader's influence extends far beyond their immediate interactions, impacting overall group morale, cohesion, and productivity. In successful teams, leaders don't just dictate; they inspire a collective purpose, acknowledging the individual strengths within the group and fostering an environment where everyone feels valued and motivated. This kind of leadership isn't about being in charge but about empowering others to contribute meaningfully, leading to enhanced group dynamics and better decision-making overall.

Influential Leadership Styles

Leadership within groups is not a one-size-fits-all concept. Influential leadership styles are diverse and have a profound impact on group dynamics. They significantly affect how groups operate, how decisions are made, and the overall morale and productivity of the team.

Understanding these styles is crucial for anyone looking to harness the power of group behavior effectively.

One of the most well-known leadership styles is transformational leadership. Transformational leaders inspire and motivate their team members to exceed their own expectations and embrace change. They create a vision of the future that is both compelling and achievable, instilling in their followers a sense of purpose and excitement. By focusing on personal growth and development, transformational leaders encourage their teams to innovate and strive for excellence.

In contrast, transactional leadership is more focused on structure, day-to-day operations, and achieving specific, immediate goals. Transactional leaders emphasize discipline and order, using rewards and penalties to motivate team members. This style is particularly effective in environments where procedures need to be followed strictly, ensuring that tasks are completed efficiently and deadlines are met. While it may not be as inspirational, transactional leadership provides the clarity and stability some teams require to function at their best.

Another impactful style is democratic leadership, where leaders engage team members in the decision-making process. This participative approach fosters a sense of ownership and accountability within the group, as members feel their opinions are valued and considered. Democratic leadership encourages open communication and collaboration, leading to a more cohesive and motivated team. However, it requires leaders to be patient and adept at facilitating discussions, ensuring that the decision-making process remains productive and focused.

Laissez-faire leadership takes a hands-off approach, granting team members a high degree of autonomy in how they accomplish their tasks. This style can be highly effective for teams composed of skilled, self-motivated individuals who thrive on independence and creative freedom. However, its success is contingent on the team's ability to self-organize and remain disciplined without active oversight. Laissez-faire leadership can catalyze innovation, but it also poses a risk of groups losing direction if not properly managed.

Charismatic leadership shares some similarities with transformational leadership in terms of the ability to inspire and energize followers. Charismatic leaders exude confidence and passion, often wielding their magnetic personalities to rally support and drive change. They rely heavily on their distinct presence and emotional appeal to influence team members, sometimes leading to highly cohesive groups. Nevertheless, there is a potential pitfall—over-reliance on personal charisma can lead to challenges if the leader's vision isn't aligned with the group's core objectives or if it stifles diverse perspectives.

Servant leadership flips traditional hierarchies on their head by placing the leader in a supportive role to the team. This style focuses on meeting the needs of team members, fostering an environment of empowerment and trust. Servant leaders prioritize the growth and well-being of individuals, emphasizing collaboration and mutual respect. By creating a nurturing environment, these leaders build a solid foundation for long-term success. Their focus on the growth of others often results in a more loyal and dedicated team willing to go above and beyond.

The situational leadership model offers a more fluid approach, adapting leadership style to the maturity and competence of team members and the specifics of the task at hand. This flexibility allows leaders to tailor their approach, providing more direction and support as needed. Situational leaders assess factors such as the group's experience, motivation, and the complexity of tasks when deciding how best to lead. By responding to the needs of the moment, situational leaders can optimize team performance across different contexts, though it requires a keen sense of awareness and adaptability.

Another noteworthy style is visionary leadership. Visionary leaders articulate a clear direction for the future and work tirelessly to bring their vision to fruition. They emphasize strategic planning and blueprinting a future state, motivating teams by demonstrating how their roles contribute to the larger picture. This style is instrumental in steering groups through periods of significant change or when navigating uncharted territory, providing the optimism and focus needed to drive toward ambitious goals.

Applying these leadership styles effectively requires a deep understanding of both the leader's own attributes and the unique characteristics of their team. No style is inherently superior to another—each has its strengths and suitable contexts. The key is for leaders to identify which style fits best with their personal strengths while considering the needs and dynamics of the group. By doing so, leaders can create an environment where their teams are not only effective but also engaged, resilient, and prepared to tackle future challenges.

Ultimately, influential leadership isn't just about adopting a predefined style; it's about being mindful of the interplay between one's approach and the group's dynamics. Successful leaders are those who blend various elements from different styles, creating a unique strategy that leverages their team's strengths and addresses its weaknesses. Through understanding and flexibility, leaders can cultivate groups that not only achieve their short-term objectives but also grow and adapt over time.

In conclusion, understanding and deploying the right influential leadership style is a powerful tool in guiding and enhancing group dynamics. Leaders who master the art of knowing when to lead from the front, when to delegate, and how to engage the collective will of their team will find that they're poised to unlock exceptional results and inspire greatness in their groups.

The Impact of Leadership on Group Dynamics

Leadership plays a pivotal role in shaping the dynamics of any group. Whether it's a corporate team, a community project, or an informal group, the presence and style of leadership significantly influence how group members interact, make decisions, and ultimately achieve their goals. A leader is not just a figurehead; they are the catalyst that can drive a group toward either success or stagnation.

At the heart of group dynamics is the complex interplay between the leader and the group members. A leader's vision and behavior often set the tone for the group's culture. Consider a leader who exemplifies transparency and openness; they naturally foster an environment where members feel safe to express their ideas and opinions. This encourages open communication and collaboration, key characteristics of a productive group dynamic.

Leadership styles can vary significantly, each bringing different impacts on group dynamics. Authoritarian leaders, for instance, may maintain tight control over decision-making, resulting in highly disciplined but potentially less innovative groups. On the other hand, a democratic leader prioritizes input from the group, which can lead to higher member satisfaction and a stronger sense of ownership over group outcomes. Transformational leaders inspire and motivate group members by creating a compelling vision of the future, fostering high levels of commitment and driving significant change.

Much of the impact of leadership on group dynamics can be seen in how it influences group roles. Leaders have the task of clearly defining roles and responsibilities, which helps to avoid confusion and overlap that can lead to conflict or redundancy. By establishing clear roles, leaders provide structure, which is crucial for coordinated group efforts. Furthermore, when leaders acknowledge and value individual contributions, they foster a sense of belonging and competence among team members.

Effective leaders understand the importance of developing trust within the group, a fundamental element of successful dynamics. Trust strengthens bonds among members, encourages the sharing of ideas, and supports risk-taking, which can lead to innovative solutions. Leaders who consistently demonstrate integrity and fairness build an environment where trust can thrive, directly impacting the efficiency and cohesion of the group.

Another critical aspect of leadership impact is conflict resolution. In any group, conflicts are inevitable, but the way they're managed can either disrupt the group or bring about growth. A skilled leader can turn conflict into an opportunity for learning and improvement by navigating differences in a way that respects all voices. By modeling calmness, empathy, and solution-focused thinking, leaders can help the group move past disputes and emerge stronger.

Leadership also affects group dynamics through the setting and communication of goals. Clear and inspiring goals provide a sense of direction and purpose, aligning group efforts towards a common objective. Leaders who articulate and exemplify these goals enable group members to understand how their individual efforts contribute to the larger mission. This alignment motivates and energizes the group, enhancing overall performance and satisfaction.

Moreover, the emotional atmosphere within a group is largely influenced by the leader's emotional intelligence. Leaders who are empathetic, self-aware, and adept at managing emotions can create a positive emotional climate that enhances group morale. They can recognize when morale is low and take steps to uplift the group, whether through verbal encouragement, recognition of achievements, or fostering opportunities for members to connect and support each other.

The adaptability of leadership is another crucial factor affecting group dynamics. In an ever-evolving environment, leaders must be flexible and willing to adjust their strategies to meet the group's changing needs. This could involve shifting leadership styles or reorganizing group processes to improve efficiency and effectiveness. Adaptable leaders are not attached to a single method; they evolve as the group evolves, always aiming to optimize the group's potential.

Ultimately, the impact of leadership on group dynamics is profound and multifaceted. It shapes the way groups function, make decisions, and achieve objectives. By understanding and leveraging these impacts, leaders can foster an environment where group dynamics enhance performance, creativity, and satisfaction, equipping the group to overcome challenges and seize opportunities in pursuit of collective goals.

Through thoughtful and intentional leadership, the potential of a group is not just realized but multiplied, creating a powerful force capable of achieving great things. Leaders who embrace this responsibility with awareness and skill not only steer their groups toward success but also contribute to the growth and development of each group member. The interplay between leadership and group dynamics is, therefore, not just about achieving tasks but cultivating a thriving community where each member can excel and contribute meaningfully.

Chapter 5:
Communication Within Groups

Effective communication sits at the heart of successful group interactions, acting as both the fuel and the framework for collaborative endeavors. Within groups, communication forms intricate networks of exchange where ideas are not just shared but built upon, creating pathways to innovation and collective understanding. The dynamics of these interactions often determine the synergy of the team, as well as its ability to adapt and grow in the face of challenges. Overcoming barriers to communication—be it physical separation in remote teams or cultural divides in diverse groups—is paramount. It requires not just strategic approaches but a genuine openness to listen and adapt. Implementing purposeful communication strategies can transform groups, enabling them to not only exchange information effectively but to empathize, energize, and ultimately excel together. It is through nuanced communication that groups unlock their potential, transforming individual contributions into a cohesive, compelling narrative of shared success.

Effective Group Communication Strategies

Communication is the lifeline of any group or team. Without effective communication strategies, groups can stumble, falter, and miss opportunities for growth and success. In this section, we will explore several strategies that are instrumental in ensuring fruitful communication within groups. These strategies not only facilitate the sharing of ideas and information but also enhance mutual understanding and collaboration among group members, ultimately bolstering the group's overall effectiveness. Given the nuanced nature of group interactions, applying a range of communication strategies can help cater to diverse needs and dynamics within a group.

One foundational strategy is active listening. It sounds simple, but active listening requires effort and practice. We must listen not just to reply, but to understand the speaker's perspective fully. This involves paying attention to non-verbal signals such as body language and tone of voice, which often convey more than words alone. By focusing on what others are saying, without planning our response, we create a space for open dialogue. This openness encourages group members to voice their thoughts and concerns, knowing they'll be heard, fostering a culture of trust and respect.

Open and transparent communication is equally important. This means sharing relevant information freely and honestly with the group. Transparency ensures that all team members are on the same page and that decisions are made with the most complete information available. It prevents misunderstandings and the development of cliques, which can arise when information is withheld or inconsistently shared among different group members. Leaders play a key role here by modeling honesty and openness, setting the tone for the rest of the group.

Utilizing a shared language or set of terms can also greatly enhance communication within groups, particularly those that are interdisciplinary or culturally diverse. Establishing a common vocabulary mitigates misunderstanding and allows group members to communicate complex ideas more effectively. This involves co-creating a glossary of key terms and concepts that are understood broadly and deeply by each group member, thus ensuring everyone is on the same page regardless of their background or discipline.

Regular feedback sessions form another critical component of effective communication strategies. Constructive feedback helps group members understand their strengths and areas for improvement. When feedback loops are established, they stimulate growth, enhance performance, and prevent issues from festering. It's essential that feedback be given thoughtfully, focusing on behavior and outcomes rather than personal attributes, to maintain a supportive and developmental environment. Receiving feedback graciously is equally important, as it demonstrates openness to change and commitment to personal improvement.

Conflict management is inherently tied to communication strategies within groups. Disagreements are natural, but when managed effectively, they can drive innovation and deeper understanding. Establishing clear guidelines for resolving conflicts helps in directing discord into productive discussions rather than allowing it to simmer unresolved. Techniques such as mediation and facilitated communication can be employed to navigate through the stormy waters of group conflicts, transforming potential obstacles into opportunities for consensus and creativity.

Utilizing diverse communication channels is increasingly significant, especially in today's dynamic environments. Depending on the group's needs and preferences, various tools—from face-to-face meetings and conference calls to emails and messaging apps—can be employed. Selecting the right communication tool for different kinds of messages improves efficiency and ensures that everyone remains informed and engaged. Moreover, these channels should be assessed regularly to ensure they're meeting the group's evolving needs.

Inclusivity is a cornerstone of effective group communication strategies. Making communication accessible to all group members, regardless of their language skills, physical abilities, or cultural backgrounds is crucial. This could mean providing interpreters, using simple and clear language, or being mindful of cultural norms around communication styles. Emphasizing inclusivity ensures that diverse perspectives are brought to the table and that every group member feels valued and empowered to contribute.

Group communication benefits vastly from establishing clearly defined roles and responsibilities. Knowing who is responsible for what within a group minimizes the potential for overlap and misunderstandings. It also ensures that everyone is accountable for their tasks, preventing bottlenecks and improving overall group efficiency. Clear definitions of roles within the group help in keeping communication focused and directed, as members understand their areas of influence and contribution.

As we delve deeper into these strategies, it's essential not to forget the role of empathy in communication. Empathetic communication bridges the gap between group members, fostering a greater sense of connection and collaboration. By practicing empathy, groups can ensure that all interactions are grounded in understanding and compassion, leading to softer conflicts and more harmonious group dynamics.

Finally, practicing adaptability in communication ensures that a group can adjust its methods and strategies as required by changing circumstances. Being flexible allows the group to stay responsive to internal shifts, such as changes in group composition or external challenges like technological advancements. This adaptability prepares the group to effectively navigate through uncertainties and seize opportunities for innovation and growth.

Incorporating these effective communication strategies into group dynamics requires commitment and repetition, but the effort reaps substantial rewards. Not only do these practices enhance the clarity and quality of information exchange, but they also foster an environment conducive to creativity, innovation, and mutual support.

Whether in workplaces, communities, or academic settings, mastering these strategies equips groups with the tools needed to surmount challenges and achieve collective goals with greater harmony and efficiency.

Overcoming Barriers to Communication

Communication within groups is the lifeblood of effective teamwork, yet it is often fraught with barriers that hinder understanding. These barriers can stem from a variety of sources, including individual differences, cultural backgrounds, and organizational dynamics. Addressing these issues head-on is key to unlocking a group's full potential.

First, let's examine the nature of these barriers. Miscommunication often arises from individual differences, such as varying communication styles. Some group members may prefer direct and concise exchanges, while others lean towards a more detailed and expressive approach. These differences can lead to misunderstandings unless they are recognized and managed proactively. Awareness and respect for each member's unique style can pave the way for more harmonious interactions.

It's imperative that group leaders encourage open dialogue. By fostering an environment where team members feel comfortable expressing their thoughts without fear of judgment, leaders can break down walls of silence. This involves actively listening to group members, providing feedback, and valuing each person's contribution.

Another significant barrier is the influence of cultural diversity. As globalization brings together people from varied backgrounds, cultural nuances become a robust variable in team interactions. For instance, what is deemed as respectful communication in one culture might be perceived as passive or assertive in another. Bridging this gap requires cultural sensitivity and an inclusive mindset.

Strategies to mitigate cultural barriers include cultural competency training and regular team-building activities that emphasize cross-cultural awareness. Such initiatives can enhance mutual understanding and create a united group identity above cultural differences. Every team member should feel their cultural background is an asset to the team's collective goal.

Organizational factors also play a critical role in either facilitating or blocking effective communication. Hierarchical structures, for example, can stymie the free flow of ideas if group members feel constrained by power distances. Encouraging a more horizontal communication structure can empower team members, making them feel more open to sharing insights and opinions.

Furthermore, technology serves as both a bridge and a hurdle in communication. While digital tools can connect remote team members, they can also lead to information overload and misinterpretation if not used judiciously. Establishing clear guidelines on the use of communication platforms can help streamline interactions and reduce misunderstandings.

Moreover, the potential for language barriers is heightened in multinational teams. Even when teams share the same official language, variations in dialect and terminology can cause confusion. Teams can overcome this by standardizing communication language and maintaining a glossary of terms that might be misinterpreted.

Emotional barriers are another less obvious obstacle to seamless communication. Personal biases or emotional states can distort the way information is both sent and received. It's crucial for teams to foster emotional intelligence and create space for empathy in their interactions, ensuring that feelings are addressed in an open and constructive manner.

Various cognitive biases also impede effective communication. Confirmation bias, for instance, might lead group members to favor information that confirms their preconceptions, dismissing critical perspectives that contradict their views. Raising awareness about these biases and incorporating practices to check them—like encouraging diverse viewpoints—can curtail their impact.

To tackle these issues, teams should implement communication protocols that include holding regular check-ins, using structured agendas in meetings, and employing feedback loops to clarify and confirm shared understanding. Such practices can enhance transparency and ensure that everyone is on the same page.

Additionally, assertiveness training can empower group members to articulate ideas clearly and respectfully, reducing instances where voices go unheard. Efforts to develop both verbal and nonverbal communication skills can further facilitate interaction, as nonverbal cues often go unnoticed in virtual settings.

Finally, celebrating and reinforcing shared successes can strengthen bonds among team members, gradually lowering communication barriers. When teams take pride in their collaborative achievements, they are more likely to engage openly and supportively with one another.

Overcoming communication barriers within groups is an evolving journey, requiring sustained effort and commitment. But with the right tools and mindset, teams can transform these challenges into opportunities for growth and innovation. By recognizing the unique contributions of each member and cultivating an environment of respect and transparency, groups can harness their collective strengths for enhanced collaboration and success.

Chapter 6:
Building Trust in Teams

Trust forms the invisible backbone of any successful team, fostering an environment where members feel safe to express their ideas, take risks, and collaborate effectively. It's not just about reliability; at its core, trust involves vulnerability, authenticity, and an unwavering belief that teammates have each other's best interests at heart. This foundation is crucial as it encourages openness and fosters a climate where innovation thrives. When individuals trust their team, they're more likely to engage in problem-solving collaboratively and support each other in the face of challenges. Cultivating this trust requires consistent and genuine communication, shared goals, and a mutual respect that transcends individual differences. By embracing these principles, teams can transform from mere groups of individuals into dynamic, cohesive units capable of achieving remarkable results together.

The Foundations of Trust

At the heart of every successful team lies a crucial element: trust. Without it, even the most talented groups can struggle to reach their full potential. But what exactly is trust, and why is it so essential for team dynamics? Trust isn't just a single attribute; it's a complex weave of reliability, transparency, and mutual respect among team members. To build a solid foundation of trust, these elements must interact cohesively, fostering a culture where individuals feel safe to express their ideas and make mistakes without fear of retribution.

Trust begins with clarity. Members of a team need to understand each other's goals and motivations. When everyone is on the same page, it's easier to establish expectations and align personal objectives with the team's larger mission. This kind of alignment helps break down silos within the group and encourages open communication. In turn, open communication facilitates transparency, a vital component of trust. When transparency becomes the norm, it minimizes uncertainties and reduces misunderstandings, allowing teams to operate smoothly even under pressure.

Consider, for example, a project team embarking on a complex initiative. The initial stages of project planning provide a critical opportunity for team leaders to set the tone for trust. Clear communication from the outset—about roles, responsibilities, and expectations—lays a foundation upon which trust can be built. It's about setting the stage for collaboration by ensuring everyone knows where they fit and why their contributions are valuable. This clarity prevents assumptions and miscommunication that could otherwise erode trust.

Once clarity is established, reliability cements the foundation of trust. Reliability means members can count on each other to fulfill commitments and deliver quality work on time. It's essential for reducing anxiety and building confidence in the team's ability to achieve its goals. When team members know they can rely on one another, they're more likely to take risks and share innovative ideas, because they trust that their peers will support them.

However, reliability is a two-way street. It requires both team leaders and members to deliver on promises consistently. A leader who models reliability sets an example for the team, demonstrating that commitments are to be honored. This behavior instills a team ethos where members uphold each other to high standards of accountability, not out of obligation, but through a mutual desire to succeed together. The more reliable the team members, the stronger the trust bond becomes.

Respect, meanwhile, is a critical, albeit often understated, pillar in the foundation of trust. Building and maintaining respect involves recognizing and valuing each member's input, regardless of their role or status. Creating a culture of respect means actively listening to differing opinions and giving credit where it's due. Such respect nourishes a sense of belonging and inclusivity, crucial for a team's cohesion. When individuals feel respected, they are more inclined to respect others, reinforcing the team's collective trust.

In many cases, mutual respect can bridge the gap between diverse personalities and styles that naturally occur within teams. Conflicts may arise, but a foundation of respect allows those disagreements to be navigated constructively, without threatening the team's cohesion. This requires ongoing effort and intentionality to ensure respect remains a constant in every interaction. From acknowledging achievements to constructively addressing failures, every action taken in respect strengthens the team's trust.

Building trust also means creating an environment that supports vulnerability. For many, vulnerability might feel like a risk, but it's a necessary ingredient for deeper trust. When team members feel they can be vulnerable—express uncertainties, share ideas that may not be fully formed, or admit mistakes—they do so because they trust their colleagues to support rather than judge them. This level of psychological safety is a hallmark of high-trust teams. Cultivating such safety involves encouraging empathy and compassion, letting members know they are valued for who they are, not just their output.

Take for example a scenario where a team faces unexpected setbacks. A member might feel responsible and hesitant to share this information, fearing repercussions. In a high-trust environment, that same individual would feel confident to voice their concerns, knowing they'd be met with understanding and collaborative problem-solving. Trust, in this context, transforms potential crises into opportunities for growth and innovation.

It's important to note that trust is not static. It evolves over time with each interaction and decision the team experiences. Therefore, maintaining trust requires ongoing commitment and attention. Regular check-ins and feedback sessions can do wonders in nurturing this environment. These practices help teams identify and address issues proactively, reinforcing trust as a living, breathing part of their dynamics.

Crucially, when it comes to trust, actions speak louder than words. Verbal affirmations are important, but it's the consistent demonstration of trust-building behaviors that truly solidifies this foundation. Acts of integrity, honesty, and transparency must align with the spoken commitments to truly nurture trust. Team leaders play an invaluable role here too; their behavior often sets the standard for the rest of the group.

As we dig deeper into strategies for cultivating trust, remember that fitting trust into a team's culture is not about implementing a one-size-fits-all solution. Every team is unique, with its own dynamics and history. The key is to remain flexible, empathetic, and dedicated to creating a robust environment where trust can flourish. This adaptability ensures that as teams evolve, trust remains an integral part of their framework, underpinning their journey toward collective success.

Strategies for Cultivating Trust

Trust is the bedrock of any successful team. It's the invisible thread that connects team members, allowing them to work together towards a common goal. When trust exists within a team, communication flows more freely, ideas are exchanged more openly, and collaboration becomes a natural process. But how do you cultivate this essential ingredient?

One key strategy is establishing a foundation of transparency. Being open about intentions, decisions, and even uncertainties can greatly enhance mutual trust. Leaders and team members alike should prioritize honesty in their interactions. This means keeping team members informed and not withholding information that could affect them. It creates an environment where everyone feels valued and integral to the operation of the team.

Another approach involves fostering a safe space for vulnerability. Teams can benefit immensely when members feel comfortable expressing their thoughts and feelings without fear of judgment or reprisal. Encouraging vulnerability requires patience and understanding, but the payoff is significant. As individuals share more of themselves, they become more connected to each other, understanding motivations and perspectives that might have otherwise remained hidden.

Encouragement and recognition play pivotal roles in nurturing trust. Simple acknowledgments of effort and achievements can bridge gaps among team members. Recognizing the contributions of others not only boosts morale but also reinforces their trust in the group's collective capability. It shows appreciation for diverse perspectives which in turn, strengthens team cohesion. This lays the groundwork for deeper trust as individuals see their value reflected in their team's success.

Consistency is another critical factor in trust-building. Teams thrive when predictability and reliability underlie their interactions. When team members know that they can rely on each other for support, advice, and accountability, trust grows naturally. However, it's not just about consistency in actions but also in values and principles. Acting in accordance with declared priorities and adhering to collective norms communicates integrity, further solidifying trust.

Open dialogue fosters curiosity and understanding among team members. Encouraging questions, promoting healthy debate, and allowing differing opinions can all enrich a team's work. In such environments, challenges to one's thinking become opportunities for learning, rather than threats. This openness not only cultivates trust but also stimulates innovation and growth as teams navigate complex dynamics together.

Empowerment offers another path to trust-building. Providing team members with the autonomy to pursue their tasks and make decisions conveys faith in their abilities. When people feel trusted to take responsibility, they're likely to reciprocate by trusting the intentions and competencies of others. However, empowerment must come with support; guiding individuals while allowing room for independent problem-solving can significantly bolster the trust quotient in a team.

Conflict, while often perceived negatively, can also present unique opportunities for trust-building if handled appropriately. Encouraging resolution through honest and constructive discussions can demystify conflicts and allow team members to unveil their underlying issues. Effective conflict resolution necessitates listening deeply, articulating feelings clearly, and striving for solutions that satisfy all parties involved. Successfully navigating conflicts can reveal shared values and strengthen interpersonal bonds.

Nurturing trust is not a one-time effort but requires continuous dedication. Regular reflection, feedback, and adaptation are vital to maintaining the health of any team. Engaging in regular team reflections and inviting feedback can help identify areas where trust might be faltering. Addressing these issues promptly demonstrates a commitment to maintaining a trust-rich environment and encourages ongoing growth.

Finally, trust is strongest in a culture that values diversity and inclusivity. Embracing varied perspectives invites broader thinking and acceptance. It's crucial to recognize and challenge unconscious biases that may hinder fostering trust across diverse team members. Encouraging diversity in thought, background, and skills enriches team dialogues, leading to holistic and innovative solutions to complex problems.

In conclusion, cultivating trust in teams requires deliberate efforts and practices. Ensuring transparency, promoting vulnerability, providing recognition and consistency, engaging in open dialogue, encouraging empowerment, and constructively handling conflicts can all significantly contribute to a trustworthy team environment. As teams continuously nurture these strategies, they not only build robust trust but also foster collaboration that can propel them towards their shared goals with greater solidarity and effectiveness.

Chapter 7:
Conflict Resolution in Teams

Conflict in teams, while often perceived as detrimental, can actually be a catalyst for growth and innovation when managed effectively. Understanding the roots of conflict is crucial for turning potential disruptions into opportunities for strengthening team ties and enhancing performance. Conflicts can emerge from various sources, such as differences in values, communication breakdowns, or competition for resources. To navigate these challenges, teams must embrace open and honest communication, fostering a culture where diverse perspectives are not only welcomed but leveraged. Effective conflict management involves recognizing emotions, encouraging empathy, and actively engaging in problem-solving techniques that focus on the interests of all parties involved. When team members feel heard and respected, they are more likely to collaborate towards a collective resolution, ultimately transforming conflict into a shared learning experience that propels the team forward. Encouraging a mindset that sees conflict as an opportunity, rather than an obstacle, empowers teams to harness their collective potential, driving both innovation and cohesion.

Identifying Sources of Conflict

Understanding the roots of conflict within teams is crucial for leaders and members alike. Conflicts often emerge from a complex web of interpersonal dynamics, differing goals, and varying perspectives.

Grasping these sources isn't just about resolving issues as they arise; it's about fostering an environment where diverse viewpoints are acknowledged and valued, ultimately leading to innovative solutions and cohesive teamwork.

A primary source of conflict lies in differing values and beliefs. Each team member brings their unique background, often shaped by personal experiences, culture, and education. These differences can enrich a team's creative potential, yet they also set the stage for misunderstandings and conflicts. An individual's cultural norms might conflict with another's, leading to disagreements on the best practices or approaches for achieving team goals.

Role ambiguity can also sow the seeds of discord. When team roles and responsibilities are not clearly defined, members may have conflicting understandings of what is expected from each other. This misunderstanding can lead to frustration and inefficiency, as individuals duplicate efforts or, worse, essential tasks fall through the cracks. Establishing clear objectives and defining each member's role can prevent such friction from escalating into full-blown disputes.

Moreover, communication—or lack thereof—serves as a significant conflict catalyst. Poor communication can result in gaps in knowledge, misinformation, and a lack of feedback. When team members aren't communicating effectively, assumptions arise, leading to misinterpretations. Encouraging open and transparent communication can bridge these gaps, ensuring that everyone is on the same page and working towards common goals.

Personality clashes are another frequent source of conflict. In any team, individuals with diverse personality types must collaborate closely. While some may approach tasks analytically, others might rely on intuition or emotions. While such diversity can be beneficial, it also presents a potential for conflict. Recognizing and appreciating these differences and utilizing tools like personality assessments can aid teams in navigating and harmonizing these divergent styles.

Resource scarcity also contributes to tension within teams. Limited resources—be it time, budget, or materials—often create competition among team members, as each strives to secure what they need for their projects. This competition can devolve into conflict if not managed wisely. Leaders can mitigate these issues by setting realistic expectations and facilitating resource allocation that reflects the team's priorities and capabilities.

Additionally, past experiences and history play a role in conflict emergence. Team members who have worked together before may carry over unresolved issues or grievances from previous interactions. These lingering tensions can create a fragile team dynamic, where minor disagreements quickly escalate. Addressing past conflicts directly and fostering a culture of forgiveness and growth can help reconcile these historical differences.

Power dynamics within a team can be a subtle yet powerful source of conflict. Teams often have informal hierarchies based on expertise, tenure, or even personality. When these dynamics lead to an imbalance where certain voices are consistently prioritized over others, frustrations and disagreement grow. Acknowledging the existence of such dynamics and striving for an inclusive environment where every contribution is valued can help in mitigating power-related conflicts.

Conflicting goals, whether between individuals or departments, are another conflict source. Teams working in a larger organizational context may find their objectives at odds with those of other units. Misalignment in goals can produce tension as team members struggle to meet their aims while accommodating others. Facilitating regular alignment meetings and ensuring that all team goals feed into the broader organizational mission can relieve such tensions.

Stress and high-pressure environments amplify existing tensions, creating fertile grounds for conflict. When team members are under significant pressure to deliver results quickly, patience runs thin, and mistakes become more frequent. Stress management techniques and ensuring a supportive environment can help teams navigate these high-pressure situations more gracefully.

Ultimately, identifying sources of conflict is not about assigning blame. It's about understanding the intricate human dynamics at play in group settings. Addressing these sources requires empathy, patience, and a strategic approach. By identifying and resolving conflicts effectively, teams can move beyond mere coexistence to foster innovation, discover new solutions, and achieve a harmonious and productive team environment. These insights pave the way for thriving collectively, harnessing the diversity of thoughts and experiences that each member brings to the table.

Techniques for Effective Conflict Management

Conflict in teams isn't just inevitable; it's often a catalyst for growth. However, how a team manages conflict can mean the difference between crippling discord and constructive debate. Recognizing this brings us to a set of techniques designed to deftly steer disagreements towards positive outcomes. Successful conflict management isn't about avoiding disputes altogether but transforming them into opportunities for clearer communication and enhanced understanding. So, let's delve into these techniques that can aid teams in harnessing conflict effectively.

An essential first step is **creating a safe environment** for open communication. When team members feel secure expressing divergent opinions without fear of ridicule or retribution, the foundation for constructive conflict is laid. Leaders play a pivotal role in fostering this atmosphere; they should encourage transparency and model active listening. By acknowledging different perspectives and valuing contributions, leaders can demystify the perception that conflict equates to failure.

Next is the practice of **active listening**, one of the more underrated yet impactful skills in conflict management. Active listening involves more than just hearing words—it requires understanding the emotions and intentions behind them. This can be achieved by maintaining eye contact, nodding in agreement, or offering verbal affirmations like "I see your point." Additionally, asking open-ended questions furthers the dialogue and helps clarify points of contention, making it easier to identify the root cause of a conflict.

Another technique involves *empathy*—the ability to place oneself in another's shoes. Empathy bridges the gap between conflicting parties, fostering a sense of understanding and respect, even in disagreement. By acknowledging the feelings and viewpoints of others, team members can navigate conflicts with increased sensitivity, often reaching compromises that consider all parties' needs. This approach not only resolves the current disagreement but also strengthens team bonds, promoting a more harmonious working environment.

Tied closely to empathy is the art of **finding common ground**. In any conflict, some commonalities often get overlooked amidst the differences. Teams that focus on shared goals or values can use those as a foundation to resolve disagreements. Identifying these commonalities helps realign perspectives towards collaborative solutions where every member feels invested in the outcome. The goal isn't to diminish differing views but to highlight that they can coexist within the broader scope of the team's objectives.

An effective technique in conflict management is setting clear **boundaries and rules** for engagement. Establishing guidelines early, such as time limits for speaking or prohibiting interrupting, can prevent discussions from spiraling into chaotic arguments. These parameters provide structure, ensuring that team discussions remain respectful and productive. Clear rules of engagement signify that while all voices will be heard, the focus remains on finding a solution rather than highlighting personal victories.

Utilizing a **neutral third-party facilitator** can be advantageous, especially when conflicts escalate beyond the team's ability to self-manage. A facilitator can guide the discussion neutrally, giving equal expression opportunity to all sides. They can also introduce unbiased perspectives that might highlight overlooked solutions. This impartial approach encourages fairness and reduces the emotional intensity of conflicts, allowing for more rational and objective resolution processes.

Another useful approach involves the technique of **brainstorming solutions**. Encouraging team members to collaboratively generate solutions to the problem at hand can transform conflict into a creative challenge. By shifting focus from what's wrong to what can be done, teams rediscover their collaborative strengths. It fosters a problem-solving mindset, invoking innovation and creativity in addressing the issues causing conflict. Importantly, this method does not discount existing disagreements but uses them as a springboard for innovative thinking.

Regular **feedback loops** accentuate conflict management strategies. Constructive feedback, delivered promptly, keeps team dynamics fluid and responsive. Frequent team check-ins can help nip potential conflicts in the bud by addressing emerging issues before they escalate. This method also empowers individuals by giving them voice and accountability in their contributions to the team's environment, thus reinforcing a proactive culture of conflict management.

It's also imperative to cultivate an understanding of **cultural differences** within a team. Diversity brings various viewpoints but can also lead to misunderstandings. Encouraging an awareness of cross-cultural communication norms can reduce friction, enabling team members to respect differences while working synergistically. Workshops or training sessions on cultural sensitivity can be incredibly beneficial, allowing team members to appreciate and leverage the diversity of perspectives in the room.

Finally, understanding the role of **emotion management** in conflicts can not be overstated. Emotions often run high during disagreements, clouding judgment and escalating tensions. Encouraging team members to engage in emotion regulation tactics—such as mindfulness, taking breaks during heated exchanges, or employing calming techniques—can prevent emotions from steering the conflict away from a constructive path.

The journey of mastering effective conflict management techniques is ongoing, as each conflict presents new challenges and learning opportunities. By embracing these methods, teams not only navigate through conflicts more smoothly but also emerge stronger, more connected, and ready to tackle future challenges with an enhanced sense of collective strength and resilience.

Chapter 8:
Harnessing Diversity in Groups

In today's interconnected world, harnessing diversity within groups isn't just an ethical imperative but a strategic advantage that can significantly enhance creativity and problem-solving. Embracing diverse perspectives allows teams to view challenges through multiple lenses, fostering innovative solutions that might otherwise be overlooked. However, realizing this potential demands deliberate strategies to ensure every voice is heard and valued. By cultivating an inclusive environment where members can openly share their unique insights and experiences, teams can transform differences into strengths. This approach not only enriches group understanding but also strengthens resilience against biases and stagnation. Ultimately, when diversity becomes integral to group identity, it propels individuals towards a collective goal, harmonizing their varied approaches into a powerful, unified trajectory.

The Benefits of Diverse Teams

The contemporary workplace often reflects a tapestry of varied cultures, backgrounds, and perspectives. This multifaceted landscape is not just a colorful mosaic; it is a treasure trove of untapped potential. *Harnessing diversity in teams* offers manifold benefits that can propel group dynamics and performance to new heights. When teams embrace diversity, they unlock doors to innovation, creativity, and superior decision-making.

First and foremost, diverse teams bring a multitude of perspectives to the table. Imagine a team with members from different cultural backgrounds, educational fields, and life experiences. Such variety fosters a broader outlook, allowing teams to tackle problems with a comprehensive lens. This expansive viewpoint is crucial in today's globalized world, where solutions often require multifaceted approaches. When team members come together, they pool their unique insights and experiences, which can spark creativity and lead to innovative solutions that homogeneous teams might overlook.

Moreover, diversity can enhance problem-solving abilities within a team. Teams with varied skill sets and knowledge bases are better equipped to approach challenges from different angles, leading to more effective and creative problem resolution. It's not just about having more ideas, but about having diverse ideas that lead to a deeper understanding of the issues at hand. Members challenge each other's assumptions and provide alternative solutions, which ultimately enhances the team's ability to solve complex problems.

Furthermore, embracing diversity improves decision-making. Teams composed of diverse individuals tend to consider a wider range of options and are less susceptible to groupthink. This broader perspective reduces the likelihood of poor decision-making based on a narrow set of ideas. Diverse groups are more apt to question the status quo and consider "what if" scenarios, leading to more thoughtful and informed decisions.

Beyond decision-making and problem-solving, diverse teams can enhance performance in measurable ways. Research has shown that inclusive teams are more productive and better at identifying and capitalizing on new opportunities. They tend to be more adaptable, quickly learning from each other and adjusting strategies to meet environmental changes.

Diversity also plays a critical role in attracting and retaining top talent. Organizations known for valuing diverse teams often stand out as employers of choice. They signal to prospective employees that fresh ideas and different viewpoints are celebrated, not stifled. When team members feel that their unique contributions are valued, it fosters a sense of belonging. This increases job satisfaction and loyalty, reducing turnover rates and enhancing team stability over time.

Effective communication is another benefit that cannot be overstated. A diverse team exposes members to different languages, communication styles, and expressions. This exposure not only improves individual communication skills but also enhances the team's ability to work effectively with external partners. Teams that can navigate this diversity successfully are often better prepared for international collaborations and dealings.

Additionally, diverse teams often enjoy richer discussions and more engaging interactions. With varying viewpoints and experiences, discussions are naturally more dynamic. Teams learn to respect each member's point of view, fostering an inclusive environment where everyone feels heard and valued. These lively discussions not only lead to innovation but also build stronger team rapport.

Contemplate the role of empathy in diverse teams. With exposure to various perspectives and backgrounds, team members can develop a deeper understanding of and respect for others, thereby cultivating empathy. This emotional intelligence is a valuable asset in all team interactions. Empathetic teams work more harmoniously, demonstrate greater collaboration, and are better positioned to support each other through challenges.

Moreover, diverse teams can foster resilience. With a mix of strengths and experiences, they are better poised to withstand setbacks. This resilience comes from the team's ability to pivot and adapt strategies quickly in response to challenges, utilizing their collective knowledge and experiences. In dynamic environments, the ability to adapt is a decisive factor for long-term success.

Finally, the societal and ethical imperative to embrace diversity should not be overlooked. In a world where equity and inclusivity are increasingly prioritized, organizations that lead in diversity set a benchmark for ethical leadership. They contribute positively to social change, demonstrating a commitment to a fairer and more inclusive world.

In conclusion, the benefits of diverse teams are profound. From enhanced creativity and improved decision-making to greater resilience and empathy, diverse groups bring unique strengths and opportunities to the table. As we continue to understand and leverage the benefits of diversity, the challenge lies not in assembling diverse teams but in unlocking their full potential. Fostering environments where diversity is embraced and valued is key—it's about harnessing this diversity to create meaningful and impactful change. The journey of diverse teams is an ongoing evolution, where learning from one another continually enhances team dynamics and achievements.

Strategies for Embracing Diversity

Diversity in groups isn't just a buzzword; it's a wealth of possibilities that can elevate group performance and innovation. Embracing diversity requires conscious actions that go beyond mere tolerance; it demands an intentional celebration and integration of various perspectives. The key lies in understanding that a diverse group is only as effective as its ability to harness the different backgrounds, experiences, and skills of its members. This section explores actionable strategies to help teams not only accept diversity but make it an intrinsic part of their collaborative fabric.

One effective strategy for embracing diversity is fostering an inclusive culture. Inclusion is the glue that holds a diverse team together. Without it, diversity loses its power. Encouraging open conversations and creating spaces where every team member feels valued and heard builds a strong foundation for inclusion. This atmosphere encourages the free exchange of ideas, where team members aren't just allowed but motivated to share their unique perspectives. When individuals feel safe expressing their thoughts without fear of judgment or retaliation, they contribute more authentically and creatively, enriching the group's output.

Leadership plays a pivotal role in driving diversity and inclusion. Leaders who model inclusive behavior—actively seeking input from all members, ensuring equitable opportunities for participation, and addressing any signs of bias—set a tone for the entire team. They can also drive diversity by championing diversity initiatives, from mentoring programs to diversity training sessions. By doing so, leaders send a clear message that inclusivity is not a checkbox exercise but a core value.

Another strategy involves education and training. Providing diversity training helps team members understand the importance of diversity and equips them with the skills to engage with it constructively. Workshops and seminars on cultural competency, unconscious bias, and inclusive communication enable team members to question their assumptions and adopt more inclusive practices. This training not only raises awareness but also promotes empathy, allowing individuals to appreciate the historical and social contexts of others' experiences.

Structured diversity initiatives such as mentorship programs and affinity groups further consolidate efforts to embrace diversity. Mentorship programs can be particularly effective, matching new or underrepresented employees with more experienced mentors who can offer guidance and support. Affinity groups allow members with shared backgrounds or interests to connect, providing a platform for dialogue and peer support. These groups often generate recommendations that can inform broader organizational strategies for diversity and inclusion.

Recruitment and hiring practices that prioritize diversity can transform the composition and dynamics of a team. By broadening recruitment channels to seek candidates from a variety of backgrounds, organizations can build more inherently diverse teams. This practice might involve partnerships with educational institutions, community organizations, or participation in diversity-focused job fairs. However, it must go hand-in-hand with an inclusive onboarding process to ensure that diverse talents are retained and integrated effectively into the team.

Encouraging diversity of thought is another crucial strategy. This involves reframing how problems are approached. Instead of defaulting to traditional solutions, diverse teams can benefit from techniques such as brainstorming sessions, where all ideas are initially considered valuable. Encouraging team members to challenge the status quo and propose out-of-the-box solutions can lead to breakthroughs in innovation and performance. It requires a culture that not only tolerates dissent but views it as a gift, an opportunity to see challenges from new angles.

Creating physical and virtual spaces that reflect diversity can also have a significant psychological impact. Offices that display multicultural artwork or support diverse dietary preferences in their cafeterias signal that diversity is respected and valued. Similarly, virtual team meetings that take into account different time zones and cultural holidays respect diversity, enhancing team cohesion and morale. These changes, though seemingly simple, contribute to a larger ethos of respect and acknowledgment.

Feedback mechanisms tailored to capture diverse perspectives can enrich team dynamics. Regular feedback loops allow team members to share their experiences and suggest improvements, fostering an environment of continuous learning and adjustment. Exploring alternative feedback methods, such as anonymous surveys, can encourage candid insights, especially from members who might feel uncomfortable voicing their opinions openly. This continuous feedback helps teams adapt and implement more inclusive practices over time.

Organizations can further their diversity ambitions by aligning them with their corporate goals and values. When diversity and inclusion are linked to the core mission of an organization, they gain importance and visibility, making it easier for employees at all levels to align their actions with these goals. Clear communication about how diversity contributes to achieving business objectives ensures it remains a priority rather than an afterthought.

Tools and technologies can also support diversity initiatives effectively. Technologies that facilitate real-time translation during meetings or allow remote participation can bridge gaps between diverse team members, ensuring everyone is included in the conversation. Leveraging social media and internal communications platforms to share diversity success stories and resources keeps diversity on the organizational agenda and engages employees in ongoing dialogue.

Finally, measuring the impact of diversity initiatives through metrics and benchmarks helps sustain commitment. By evaluating the effects of diversity strategies on team performance, innovation, employee satisfaction, and retention, organizations can identify what works and what needs reevaluation. This data-driven approach ensures accountability and continuous improvement, ensuring that diversity strategies evolve as the team and organizational context change.

In conclusion, embracing diversity within groups involves a multifaceted approach that integrates structural, behavioral, and cultural changes. The strategies discussed highlight the importance of creating an inclusive culture, educating team members, adopting inclusive practices, and measuring impact to achieve sustained benefits. The journey of embracing diversity requires an ongoing commitment, but the resulting synergy, creativity, and resilience can transform teams into powerful engines of innovation and success.

Chapter 9:
Motivation and Group Performance

Understanding the relationship between motivation and group performance is crucial for cultivating high-functioning teams. When motivated, individuals not only bring their best effort but also inspire others, creating a ripple effect that elevates the entire group's output. Various elements contribute to this dynamic, including shared goals, recognition, and the intrinsic value members find in their contributions. Leaders play a key role by aligning group objectives with personal ambitions, fostering an environment where each member feels valued and driven. Furthermore, the synergy within a motivated group can lead to enhanced collaboration, creativity, and resilience in the face of challenges. It's not just about individual incentives; the collective spirit invigorates team dynamics, ensuring that the group's performance is greater than the sum of its parts. Achieving sustained motivation requires ongoing effort and adaptation, reflecting a commitment to both personal growth and team success.

Factors Influencing Group Motivation

As we delve into the intricate world of group motivation, it's essential to understand that it's not merely about the individual's desire. Group motivation is a sophisticated blend of various influences that drive team performance. Understanding these factors is key to harnessing collective energy and achieving exceptional results.

One of the pivotal factors influencing group motivation is the clarity of the group's goals. When team members have a clear understanding of the group's objectives, their motivation levels tend to be higher. This clarity helps in aligning individual motivations with team goals, fostering a sense of purpose. It's much like setting a destination before starting a journey – everyone knows where they're headed and why. Consistent and transparent communication from leadership plays a vital role in maintaining this clarity.

Another significant influence comes from the recognition and rewards system in place within a group. Recognition doesn't always have to be extravagant; even small acknowledgments of effort can profoundly affect motivation. When team members feel valued, they become more driven to contribute to the team's success. On the flip side, a lack of recognition can lead to reduced engagement and a decline in performance. Rewards and recognition create a motivating environment, turning simple tasks into challenges to be conquered.

The cultural backdrop of the group is also an influential component. A culture of trust and psychological safety allows members to express their ideas freely without the fear of being ridiculed or ignored. This environment encourages more participation, risk-taking, and exploration of innovative solutions, which are vital to maintaining high motivation levels. Trust acts as the glue that binds members, fostering cooperation and commitment, ultimately driving motivation.

Social identity and the sense of belonging within a group can significantly impact motivation as well. When individuals connect with their group's identity, they tend to put in more effort to enhance the group's well-being. This connection to the group can be instilled and nurtured through shared experiences, rituals, and traditions that convey a unique identity. Belonging motivates individuals to work harder, knowing their contributions reflect on the whole group and, subsequently, on themselves.

The role of leadership can't be overstated in influencing group motivation. Leadership that adapts to the needs of the group and individuals within it can inspire better performance. Leaders who understand and align with the emotional and psychological needs of their team members can spark motivation that sustains even under challenging circumstances. Effective leaders don't just direct; they participate, share, and uplift.

Adding to these dynamics is the external environment in which the group operates. Factors such as economic conditions, societal expectations, and competitive pressures can affect group motivation as well. A supportive external environment acts as a buffer, offering resources and stability that keeps the group focused on its mission, whereas a hostile environment can challenge and sometimes dampen motivation. Adaptive strategies can be employed to mitigate the negative impacts of such pressures.

Work structure within the group also plays a critical role in motivation. The division of tasks and the level of autonomy granted to team members can either boost or hinder motivation. Groups that encourage creativity and allow individuals some degree of control over their work see higher levels of engagement. When people feel they have a say in how they accomplish their tasks, their intrinsic motivation is unleashed.

It's also essential to address the challenges and conflicts that naturally arise in any group setting. While conflict can sometimes be seen as a negative, managed effectively, it can also serve as a catalyst for motivation. Resolving conflicts through effective communication and problem-solving strategies keeps the team cohesive, reinstating focus and drive towards shared goals. Turning challenges into opportunities for growth can enhance a group's motivation and resilience.

Mason D. Abbott

In conclusion, understanding the factors influencing group motivation requires a multifaceted approach. It involves aligning goals, recognizing effort, nurturing a positive culture, fostering a strong sense of identity, employing adaptive leadership, navigating external challenges, designing supportive structures, and managing conflicts proactively. By addressing these areas, groups can cultivate an environment ripe for motivation, leading to enhanced performance and achievement of collective goals. The true power lies in the delicate interplay of these elements, each pushing the group towards excellence.

Enhancing Group Performance

Improving group performance isn't just about fine-tuning processes or assigning roles more efficiently; it's a holistic endeavor where motivation plays a central role. To truly enhance the performance of a group, it's crucial to understand the various elements that drive individuals to work together more effectively. At its core, motivation in a group context is about aligning personal goals with group objectives. When individuals see their effort contributing to a broader purpose, performance naturally elevates.

One of the primary drivers of improved group performance is a shared vision. This doesn't merely mean having a common goal; it's about the entire team buying into what the group is trying to achieve. A sense of purpose fuels the members' engagement and commitment. When a group knows what it's working towards and why it matters, motivation levels rise, leading to better cooperation and, ultimately, enhanced productivity.

Creating an environment that fosters open communication is another key aspect of boosting group performance. Team members need to feel safe sharing ideas, concerns, or feedback without fear of reprimand or ridicule. A culture of open communication not only increases trust within the group but also paves the way for swift problem-solving and innovative thinking. When communication barriers are broken down, each member can contribute to their full potential, which enhances overall group performance.

Additionally, recognizing and celebrating individual and team accomplishments can vastly improve group performance. When achievements are acknowledged, motivation rises, and individuals are encouraged to strive for even higher goals. Celebrations of success instill a sense of pride and belonging, reinforcing the value of each contribution. Incentives, whether in the form of praise, promotions, or even simple gestures of appreciation, can have powerful impacts, propelling the group to achieve more.

Structured feedback systems also play a pivotal role in enhancing group performance. Feedback, when given constructively, helps team members understand their strengths and areas for improvement. Teams that regularly exchange feedback are more agile and better equipped to adapt to challenges. Constructive feedback loops ensure that everyone in the group is moving in the right direction and at the right pace, contributing to the group's overall performance.

Effective leadership cannot be overlooked when seeking to enhance group performance. Leaders who demonstrate emotional intelligence and can adapt their style to the needs of their team can significantly impact motivation levels. A leader who is approachable, empathetic, and inspiring helps every team member feel valued. Such leaders can motivate individuals to push past their limits and focus their energies on the collective goals of the group.

Another critical factor is the diversity of skills and perspectives within the group. A diverse team brings a wealth of ideas and approaches that can enhance problem-solving and creativity. To fully capitalize on this diversity, group dynamics need to be nurtured carefully; ensuring that all voices are heard and ideas respected. By leveraging different perspectives, groups can come up with more innovative solutions, thereby improving their overall performance.

The physical and psychological environment in which a group operates also influences performance. A supportive workplace that prioritizes well-being enhances motivation and productivity. Access to the right tools, comfortable workspaces, and a culture that promotes work-life balance can make a massive difference in how effectively a team functions. When people feel supported and valued, they're more likely to contribute meaningfully to the group's objectives.

Furthermore, alignment between individual motivations and group goals should not be underestimated. When individuals feel that their personal ambitions align with the group's purposes, the synergy created can lead to exceptional performance. Leaders can facilitate this alignment by openly discussing the objectives and allowing team members to express their own goals, finding overlap where possible.

Finally, regular training and development opportunities can enhance group performance by keeping skills sharp and knowledge up-to-date. When team members are continually learning and growing, they bring fresh ideas and renewed enthusiasm to their work. Encouraging ongoing education nurtures a culture of continuous improvement, which can greatly influence the group's ability to perform at its best.

In conclusion, enhancing group performance is a multilayered challenge that requires attention to the motivational factors affecting team members. By focusing on shared vision, open communication, recognition, feedback, leadership, diversity, supportive environments, goal alignment, and continuous development, groups can harness the full power of their collective capabilities. Such well-functioning teams are not only more productive but also more resilient, adaptable, and fulfilled in their endeavors.

Chapter 10:
Emotional Dynamics in Groups

In the intricate tapestry of group dynamics, emotions play a pivotal role, often acting as the unseen but profoundly felt undercurrent that influences every interaction. When individuals come together, their collective emotional states can foster harmony, provoke conflict, or drive the creative energy necessary for innovation. Understanding these emotional dynamics is crucial for anyone looking to harness the true potential of a group. Emotions can act as both a cohesive force and a source of division, impacting decision-making processes, motivation, and overall group performance. Skilled leaders and team members recognize not just the overt expressions of emotion, but also the subtle cues that signal underlying emotional currents. By fostering an environment where emotional awareness and regulation are prioritized, groups can cultivate resilience, empathy, and a shared sense of purpose. This emotional intelligence within groups is not only about managing emotions effectively but also about leveraging them to enhance collaboration and achieve collective goals. As we navigate through different group settings, it becomes clear that emotions are a dynamic force that, when understood and harnessed, become instrumental in propelling groups towards success and innovation.

The Role of Emotions in Group Settings

Emotions have long been regarded as the lifeblood of human interactions; they're the invisible threads that weave through group dynamics. In any collective setting, emotions serve as both drivers and inhibitors of action, shaping how individuals connect, react, and collaborate. When people come together, their emotions intermingle, creating a unique emotional ecosystem that can significantly affect group performance and cohesion.

Within this ecosystem, emotions are a double-edged sword. Positive emotions like enthusiasm and joy can inspire creativity, enhance communication, and strengthen bonds. Conversely, negative emotions such as anger, anxiety, and jealousy can sow discord and hamper productivity. Every participant in a group brings not just their skill set but also their emotional states, which can rapidly shift due to interactions and external factors.

Consider a team gathered to brainstorm innovative solutions. The enthusiasm of a few can ignite a sense of possibility, propelling the group toward groundbreaking ideas. Conversely, if left unchecked, a single member's frustration might create a ripple effect, dampening the collective energy and thwarting creativity. Emotional contagion, the phenomenon where emotions spread like wildfire through a group, plays a crucial role in these dynamics.

Such contagion underscores the importance of emotional awareness within groups. Recognizing and understanding emotional cues can be pivotal for leaders and members alike. Leaders with high emotional intelligence can interpret these cues to steer the group toward positive outcomes. They know when to address a brewing storm or how to leverage a wave of excitement to fuel motivation.

Emotions also serve as vital signals that reveal underlying issues. A spike in anxiety might be a beacon indicating unsaid concerns or unaddressed tensions. Conversely, consistent expressions of joy and satisfaction can signal alignment and shared purpose. By being attuned to these signals, groups can proactively manage emotions to nurture a supportive environment.

Understanding the interplay of emotions in groups is particularly crucial in decision-making processes. Emotions can bias decision processes, sometimes leading to more risky or conservative outcomes based on the group's emotional climate. It's a balancing act — harness emotions to encourage bold thinking while ensuring they don't lead to hasty choices.

Moreover, emotions influence group identity and solidarity. Shared joyful experiences can enhance a sense of belonging, while shared moments of frustration can bond members against perceived common challenges. These shared emotional journeys contribute to the group's narrative, often defining its culture and ethos.

Building an emotionally intelligent group requires intentional effort. It involves creating spaces for open emotional expression and developing strategies for emotional regulation. Techniques such as mindfulness, regular debriefs, and feedback sessions can help manage the emotional milieu, ensuring it supports group objectives rather than hinders them.

In essence, groups that cultivate emotional intelligence are better positioned to handle challenges, innovate, and maintain strong interpersonal connections. They understand that emotions are not just personal experiences but collective forces that can be harnessed for greater synergy and success. The role of emotions in group settings is pivotal, yet complex, demanding ongoing attention and adaptation, but the rewards in terms of improved collaboration and performance make it a worthwhile endeavor.

Techniques for Emotional Regulation

Understanding how emotions ripple through a group is key to managing collective behavior. When individuals come together, they bring their own emotional states, which often interact and amplify within the group context. In emotionally charged situations, the group's success hinges on its ability to regulate these emotional dynamics. So, how can teams effectively harness emotions to foster positive results and mitigate potential disruptions?

One technique for emotional regulation in groups is the cultivation of mindfulness. Mindfulness encourages group members to remain aware of their emotional states and those of their peers without immediate reaction or judgment. By collectively pausing to acknowledge emotions as they arise, group members can prevent hasty actions that may disrupt group harmony. Practicing mindfulness can be as simple as taking a few minutes during meetings to engage in deep breathing or guided meditation. These practices help center the group and realign everyone's focus on shared goals.

In addition to mindfulness, active emotional labeling plays a crucial role. By explicitly identifying and verbalizing emotions, individuals can better understand their own emotional responses and those of others. Encouraging open dialogue about how team members feel promotes a culture of transparency and trust. For instance, a team member might say, "I'm feeling anxious about our project's deadline." This acknowledgment not only clarifies the individual's emotional state but also invites support and empathy from the group, paving the way for collective problem-solving.

Another vital technique is developing emotional intelligence as a group. Emotional intelligence involves the ability to perceive, understand, and manage emotions. Teams with high emotional intelligence are often more empathetic and resourceful in navigating emotional challenges. Training sessions or workshops on emotional intelligence can be invaluable. For example, role-playing exercises can simulate real-life scenarios, allowing team members to practice responding to various emotional states and developing deeper insights into each other's perspectives.

It's also important to incorporate emotional debriefing sessions, especially after high-stress events or projects. These sessions function as safe spaces where team members can express their feelings about the experience, reflect on emotional reactions, and extract learning for future endeavors. During such debriefings, the focus isn't on assigning blame but on understanding emotions constructively to devise collective strategies for moving forward.

One aspect that's often overlooked is the physical environment in which a group operates. Spaces that are comfortable, well-lit, and thoughtfully arranged can significantly influence the emotional regulation of a group. An inviting space can put individuals at ease and promote open communication, whereas a cramped and poorly-lit environment may heighten stress and emotional friction. Simple adjustments, like adding plants or rearranging seating to encourage eye contact and engagement, can subtly improve the emotional atmosphere.

Journaling is another tool that can be extremely effective in emotional regulation. Group members who reflect on their emotional states through writing can gain clarity and insight into their emotions. They can identify patterns and triggers, fostering a greater understanding of not only their responses but also the group dynamics. Sharing insights from journaling in a group setting enables members to learn from each other's experiences and jointly develop strategies to address common emotional challenges.

Finally, fostering a growth mindset within the group context can transform the way emotions are managed. When team members view emotional challenges as opportunities for growth rather than insurmountable problems, they're more likely to engage collaboratively and creatively. Encouraging a culture where mistakes are seen as learning opportunities rather than failures can diminish fear-based emotions and embolden team members to contribute more authentically.

In conclusion, effectively regulating emotions within groups demands intentionality and practice. By integrating techniques like mindfulness, emotional labeling, emotional intelligence development, debriefing, optimizing physical environments, journaling, and nurturing a growth mindset, teams can manage emotions constructively. Not only does this lead to healthier group dynamics, but it also enhances overall group performance and satisfaction, turning emotional challenges into collective strengths.

Chapter 11:
Creativity and Innovation in Teams

Teams have the potential to become powerhouses of creativity and innovation when the right environment nurtures this inherent dynamism. At the heart of fostering a culture of innovation is the deliberate encouragement of diverse perspectives and open dialogue—a process that transforms collective intelligence into groundbreaking ideas. Innovative teams are not just reactive; they actively seek out new opportunities, experimenting and embracing the inevitable stumbles along the path to discovery. To keep this creative engine running smoothly, it's crucial to dismantle barriers that stifle imagination, such as rigid hierarchies or a fear of failure. Leaders play a pivotal role in this environment by championing psychological safety, which allows members to propose bold ideas without hesitation. Through practices that stimulate curiosity and collaboration, teams can transcend conventional thinking, continuously refreshing themselves with new insights and forward-thinking solutions that propel them—and their organizations—into uncharted territories of success.

Fostering a Culture of Innovation

In an age where the pace of change is relentless, fostering a culture of innovation within teams is no longer optional—it's essential. It's about creating a fertile environment where fresh ideas can take root, grow, and ultimately transform an organization. To achieve this, leaders and team members alike must cultivate certain attitudes and behaviors that encourage creativity and experimentation.

So, how does one foster such a culture? It begins with mindset. Encouraging a growth mindset across teams means nurturing a belief that abilities and intelligence can develop over time. This approach moves away from the fixed mindset, which views talents as static. Carol Dweck, the psychologist who popularized the concept of growth mindset, emphasizes that embracing challenges, being persistent in the face of setbacks, and viewing effort as a path to mastery, are keys to cultivating innovation.

Leaders play a crucial role in this process by modeling risk-taking behaviors and demonstrating a tolerance for failure. Instead of penalizing mistakes, they should focus on extracting lessons from them. When team members see their leaders taking calculated risks and learning from failures, rather than fearing repercussions, they're more likely to mirror those behaviors, creating an environment where innovative ideas can flourish.

A diverse team is often more innovative than a homogenous one. Bringing together individuals with varied backgrounds, experiences, and perspectives fosters an inclusive environment where creative tension and constructive dissent are possible. When people feel safe to express conflicting viewpoints without fear of rejection, they can brainstorm more effectively and come to solutions that might not have been possible otherwise.

Yet, establishing psychological safety—a critical element of innovative cultures—goes beyond merely tolerating different opinions. It involves nurturing an environment where all team members feel confident to speak up and share their ideas without fear of humiliation. Amy Edmondson, a renowned scholar in organizational behavior, highlights the importance of psychological safety, noting that it allows for greater risk-taking and learning from failure.

Creating rituals that encourage creativity can also help sustain an innovative culture. These might include regular brainstorming sessions where the focus is on generating quantity rather than quality, at least initially. Such practices can break down the barriers to creativity and stimulate a free flow of ideas. By suspending judgment during initial idea-generation phases, teams can explore unconventional solutions that might otherwise be dismissed.

Innovative teams are dynamic rather than static. They are keenly aware that innovation is a continual process, not a one-time event. Feedback loops are essential; continuous reflection on both successes and failures keeps teams agile and adaptable. This adaptability is crucial because the journey from idea conception to execution is rarely linear.

Another critical component is embedding innovation into the team's metrics of success. Traditional performance indicators often focus on immediate results and efficiencies, whereas innovation might require redefining success metrics to include learning, experimentation, and long-term impact. Incentives should reflect these values, motivating team members to pursue novel and creative solutions.

The physical and virtual workspace also plays a role. Spaces that are designed to encourage interaction, movement, and creativity can stimulate innovation. Digital tools can facilitate remote collaboration and idea-sharing, breaking down geographic barriers and enabling a diverse range of inputs, which is increasingly important in today's global team setups.

Training and development shouldn't be overlooked either. Building a culture of innovation includes ensuring that team members possess not only the technical skills required for their roles but also the creative skills needed for problem-solving and innovation. Workshops on creative thinking, storytelling, and design thinking methodologies can equip team members with the tools they need to think outside the usual boundaries.

Trust is another cornerstone of an innovative culture. It underpins every interaction and decision within a team. When trust is present, communication flows freely, collaboration deepens, and teams can take risks with confidence. Leaders should focus on transparent communication and team-building activities that strengthen bonds and foster a deeper understanding among team members.

Furthermore, leaders should champion a vision that prioritizes innovation as a core value. Visions and missions serve as guiding stars that can inspire and motivate teams to push beyond their limits. They need to see how their innovative efforts tie into something larger, something meaningful. Therefore, celebrating innovation publicly within the organization can reinforce its importance and value, encouraging more team members to contribute creatively.

Lastly, it's important to note that fostering a culture of innovation requires patience and consistency. Results might not be immediate, but as the culture solidifies, the benefits compound, leading to breakthroughs in both team development and organizational success. Long-term commitment to these principles and practices can transform teams into powerhouses of creativity and innovation.

By fostering a culture of innovation, teams can not only deal with present challenges but also prepare for future opportunities and disruptions. As organizations aim to differentiate themselves in a competitive marketplace, those that embrace innovation as part of their core will lead the way.

Overcoming Creativity Blocks

In the dynamic landscape of team-based endeavors, creativity is often the lifeblood of innovation and progress. Yet, creativity isn't always forthcoming. Even the most dynamic teams occasionally encounter roadblocks. These creativity blocks can be frustrating, creating barriers that prevent innovative ideas from taking shape. Understanding how to overcome these blocks is essential for teams aspiring to be at the forefront of their fields.

One of the most common causes of creativity blocks within teams is a fear of failure. When team members are overly concerned about making mistakes, they tend to play it safe. This fear stifles creativity because bold, new ideas often come with a level of risk. It's crucial to cultivate an environment where failure is seen as a step in the learning process rather than a setback. Encouraging a mindset that values experimentation and views mistakes as opportunities for growth can help alleviate this fear.

Another significant factor that contributes to creativity blocks is excessive self-censorship. Individuals often withhold ideas they think might be dismissed or ridiculed. To combat this, teams must cultivate a culture of psychological safety, where members feel comfortable sharing any thoughts without the fear of negative judgment. Open dialogue, coupled with an emphasis on active listening, helps to ensure that all voices are heard and valued.

Time pressure is a double-edged sword in the creative process. While deadlines can provide motivation, excessive time constraints can hamper creativity by preventing deep, reflective thinking. Effective time management can mitigate this. Allocating time specifically for brainstorming sessions without the immediate pressure of deadlines allows team members to explore unconventional ideas. Scheduling regular intervals where creativity is routine rather than a rushed necessity can create a more relaxed atmosphere conducive to innovation.

Environmental factors also play a substantial role. A monotonous environment, both physically and mentally, can dampen creativity. A change of scenery or variations in routine can spur new ideas. Inviting guest speakers, introducing new methodologies, or even changing meeting locations might break the monotony, providing fresh perspectives. Small changes can reinvigorate a team's creative spirit, pushing them beyond habitual patterns of thought.

Group dynamics significantly impact a team's creative output. Teams often suffer from groupthink, where the desire for harmony results in irrational decision-making. Interrupting groupthink requires deliberately bringing diverse perspectives into discussions. Including team members from different backgrounds or involving departments not traditionally associated with the task at hand can challenge prevailing assumptions and stimulate creativity. Incorporating diverse viewpoints not only provides a broader base of ideas but also encourages critical thinking and creativity.

The role of leadership cannot be understated in overcoming creativity blocks. Leaders set the tone for what is acceptable within the team. Supportive leadership recognizes and rewards creative efforts, instilling a culture that values innovation. Successful leaders know when to step back and let their teams take the lead, providing guidance without stifling creativity. By fostering autonomy, leaders empower their teams to explore and develop unimpeded by authoritarian oversight.

Techniques such as brainwriting and mind mapping can be invaluable tools for sparking creativity. Brainwriting involves team members writing down ideas independently before sharing them. This can reduce the influence of dominant personalities in discussions and ensure that all voices are represented. Mind mapping, on the other hand, visually organizes information, helping teams see connections between ideas they might not have otherwise recognized. Such techniques provide structure without limiting creative thought.

A flexible mindset is another antidote to creativity blocks. Teams that rigidly adhere to established processes might miss innovative opportunities. Flexibility allows teams to pivot when necessary, adapting to new circumstances and insights. When team members embrace adaptability, they remain open to new ways of thinking, which is essential for overcoming barriers to creative innovation.

Creative partnerships both within and outside the team can boost innovation. Collaborating with experts from different fields or industries can impart new perspectives and insights that the team alone might not possess. These external collaborations can help a team see challenges from fresh angles and inspire solutions that might otherwise remain undiscovered.

Lastly, maintaining a balance between focused work and idle time is vital. Scientific studies repeatedly reveal the importance of downtime for fostering creativity. Breaks and leisurely activities refresh mindsets and often spark inspiration due to the subconscious processing of ideas. This balance ensures that when team members reconvene, they do so with renewed vigor and, importantly, novel insights that might have eluded them during concentrated efforts.

Overcoming creativity blocks requires a multifaceted approach that addresses emotional, cognitive, and environmental factors. By fostering a culture that supports risk-taking, embraces diverse viewpoints, and values both autonomy and collaboration, teams can navigate past these barriers. The payoff is substantial—the ability to innovate and bring to life ideas that could redefine their fields. As teams strengthen their creativity resilience, they not only overcome blocks but become architects of transformation and progress in an ever-evolving landscape.

Chapter 12:
Virtual Teams and
Remote Collaboration

A s the landscape of work rapidly transforms, virtual teams have moved from a novel concept to a predominant way of collaboration. This shift brings about distinct challenges that, if navigated thoughtfully, can lead to exceptional results. In virtual settings, the absence of physical proximity demands heightened clarity in communication and a stronger emphasis on trust. Remote teams must devise creative solutions to bridge the gap caused by lack of face-to-face interaction, nurturing a shared sense of purpose and alignment despite geographical separation. Teams thrive when they adopt best practices like establishing clear communication protocols, leveraging digital tools effectively, and promoting flexibility to accommodate diverse work styles and time zones. By mastering these strategies, virtual teams not only overcome inherent challenges but also unleash their potential to innovate and excel in today's interconnected world.

Challenges of Virtual Teams

As we enter the age of virtual teams and remote collaboration, we find ourselves encountering a unique set of challenges that traditional teams do not face. These challenges emanate from the very essence of what makes virtual teams distinct—their disconnection from the traditional, physical office space. No longer anchored by geographic proximity, virtual teams operate in a realm where physical presence is replaced by digital connection. However, this shift comes with its complexities, demanding new approaches to team dynamics and collaboration.

The first challenge arises from the lack of face-to-face interactions, which often results in misunderstandings and misinterpretations. Body language and facial expressions play critical roles in communication, contributing to how messages are perceived and understood. Without these nonverbal cues, team members must rely solely on written or verbal communication, which can be limited by tone and clarity. Even with video conferencing tools at our disposal, the nuances of body language can be lost, leading to potential friction and miscommunication among team members.

Another significant challenge is the issue of time zone differences. Virtual teams often span continents and countries, meaning that what is daytime for some may be the middle of the night for others. This can complicate scheduling and necessitate flexible working hours to accommodate teammates from different parts of the world. The overlapping work hours may be minimal, leading to delays in decision-making and project progress.

Trust is another cornerstone of effective teams that is particularly challenging to establish and maintain in a virtual setting. The absence of in-person interactions might make it harder for team members to build the rapport that often develops naturally when working side-by-side. Trust-building, in this context, requires intentional efforts and strategies, such as establishing clear communication norms and regular check-ins. Without trust, collaboration becomes stilted and team resilience diminishes.

Virtual teams also face the risk of isolation among team members. The human element of workplace camaraderie can weaken, with colleagues feeling more like isolated operators rather than parts of a cohesive team. This can impact morale, leading to decreased motivation and potentially higher turnover rates. The solution lies in creating virtual spaces for informal interactions, like casual chat groups or virtual coffee breaks, to simulate the water cooler conversations that happen in a physical office.

Technology, while enabling virtual work, can also be a double-edged sword. Technical issues, from poor internet connectivity to software glitches, can disrupt communication and workflow, creating frustration and inefficiencies. Moreover, the reliance on digital tools for collaboration requires a baseline level of tech-savviness among team members. Disparities in technological proficiency can create divides within the team, potentially exacerbating feelings of exclusion or incompetence.

Another layer of complexity arises from the potential for digital burnout. The line between work and home becomes blurred as team members navigate a world where their office is mere steps away from their living room. Constant connectivity can lead to an "always-on" mentality, reducing downtime and increasing stress levels. Managing work-life balance in such an environment becomes paramount to preventing burnout and maintaining overall team well-being.

Despite these challenges, virtual teams possess the potential to be as effective, if not more so, than traditional teams. It requires deliberate strategies to address and mitigate these obstacles. Leaders must leverage the strengths of diverse backgrounds and perspectives, encouraging open communication and fostering a culture of inclusivity. Periodic virtual meetups and recognition of accomplishments can go a long way in building team morale and cohesiveness.

Moreover, providing clear goals and roles is essential in avoiding confusion and ensuring that team members understand their contributions to the collective effort. Clarity in these areas enables virtual teams to navigate the complexities of remote work with more confidence and efficiency.

With advancements in technology and shifts in work culture, the future of virtual teams looks promising, but mindful navigation of these inherent challenges is key. As we explore best practices for remote collaboration, it's crucial that we cultivate an environment where virtual teams can thrive, harnessing the diversity, creativity, and innovation they are capable of achieving, even from afar.

Best Practices for Remote Collaboration

In today's rapidly evolving work environment, remote collaboration isn't just a trend—it's a necessity. As virtual teams become more prevalent, understanding how to collaborate effectively when team members are scattered across different locations, time zones, and even cultures becomes paramount. Successfully navigating these challenges requires intentional strategies and practices tailored for a non-traditional workspace, allowing teams to maintain the essence of face-to-face interaction while embracing the flexibility that remote work offers.

First and foremost, communication is the lifeblood of remote collaboration. Without the availability of spontaneous office interactions, such as hallway chats or lunch hour meet-ups, virtual teams must prioritize clear and frequent communication. Using a combination of synchronous and asynchronous tools can bridge the gap. Video calls help personalize interactions and should be used regularly to foster a personal connection. Meanwhile, communication platforms like Slack or Microsoft Teams allow for ongoing dialogue and quick sharing of information. The key is to establish norms around how and when different tools should be used to minimize misunderstandings and information overload.

Creating a structured communication plan can drastically improve a team's ability to function remotely. This plan should outline the expectations for responsiveness and availability, starting with daily check-ins to weekly reviews. It allows team members to feel connected and engaged, ensuring everyone is on the same page. Furthermore, establishing a shared timeline for projects can guide interactions, making members more conscious of time zone differences and respecting each other's working hours.

Trust is another cornerstone of successful remote teams. When team members aren't physically together, a certain level of autonomy in task execution becomes necessary, making trust a critical factor. It's crucial for leaders to foster an environment where team members feel their contributions are valued and that they have ownership over their work. Regular feedback sessions, both formal and informal, can help reinforce this trust by showing that leaders care about members' opinions and contributions. Trust, once established, can lead to increased productivity and a more positive group dynamic.

In addition to communication and trust, clear role definition is essential. Each team member should know their responsibilities and how their work contributes to the team's goals. This clarity helps prevent overlaps and confusions that remote environments can exacerbate. To reinforce this, project management tools like Trello or Asana can be employed to track tasks and deadlines, ensuring transparency and alignment among team members.

Another practice that impacts remote collaboration is fostering an inclusive team culture. Remote work can sometimes lead to feelings of isolation, and it's easy for virtual employees to get stuck in their silos. Leaders should be mindful of integrating social activities or virtual gatherings into regular work schedules to mitigate this risk. Whether it's a virtual coffee break, a themed meeting, or team-building exercises, fostering personal connections can simulate the water cooler conversations that are often missing in remote settings.

Given the diversity that comes with global remote teams, cultural sensitivity also plays a broader role in collaborative success. Team members might have different ways of communicating, different working styles, and varying levels of formality. Understanding and respecting these differences can prevent miscommunications and foster a harmonious working environment. Teams that appreciate diverse perspectives are often more creative and innovative, as varied viewpoints encourage broader solutions and ideas.

Moreover, leveraging technology can significantly enhance remote collaboration. From cloud-based sharing platforms like Google Drive to specialized software for real-time collaboration like Miro, technology empowers teams to work together seamlessly despite physical distance. It's crucial, though, to select tools that match the team's specific needs and to ensure that all team members are comfortable and proficient in using them.

It is also important to focus on results rather than micromanaging processes. Remote work naturally leans towards a results-oriented approach, encouraging teams to measure success by outcomes rather than hours logged. This shift can be motivating for team members, empowering them to manage their time and work in a way that best suits them, thus enhancing overall efficiency.

On an organizational level, there needs to be a commitment to continuous learning and adaptation. Remote teams operate in dynamic environments, and the practices that work today might not be effective tomorrow. Feedback loops should be incorporated into team operations to assess what's working and what isn't, allowing teams to adjust and improve their strategies. This approach not only leads to improved collaboration but also fosters a growth-oriented culture.

Finally, recognition and acknowledgment play significant roles in maintaining team morale. Remote workers can't benefit from a casual pat on the back or in-office praise, so leaders need to be intentional in how they recognize achievements and contributions. Recognizing efforts and celebrating milestones, whether big or small, can motivate team members to continue delivering high-quality work and reinforce a sense of belonging.

In conclusion, while remote collaboration presents unique challenges, it opens up a world of opportunity for innovation and flexibility. By adhering to these best practices, teams can not only survive but thrive in a remote work setting, improving productivity, cohesion, and satisfaction. The transition to remote work doesn't mean leaving traditional collaboration behind; instead, it's about evolving and adapting these practices to a virtual landscape to create high-performing, resilient teams. As these strategies take root, they reshape the future of teamwork into something that's both dynamic and inclusive.

Chapter 13:
The Impact of Technology
on Group Interactions

Chapter 13 explores the transformative role technology plays in shaping group interactions. As digital tools redefine collaboration, the impact on group dynamics is profound. Real-time communication platforms, cloud-based collaboration tools, and social networks have changed how groups connect and work together, often dissolving geographical boundaries and enabling diverse teams. These technologies enhance speed and flexibility but also introduce new challenges, such as managing digital overload and ensuring equitable participation. Groups must adapt to these shifts by fostering skills that leverage technology effectively while maintaining human connection. Navigating technological landscapes requires an understanding of its nuances to harness potential benefits without succumbing to drawbacks like miscommunication or distraction. By maintaining a balance, teams can optimize technological advances as a force to drive innovation and collective achievement.

Digital Tools for Enhanced Collaboration

In the ever-evolving landscape of team interactions, digital tools have emerged as indispensable assets for enhancing collaboration. Whether teams are co-located or geographically dispersed, technology has forged new paths for communication, creativity, and efficiency. The impact of these digital tools transcends mere convenience; they reshape how teams function, creating opportunities and challenges that demand mindful navigation.

At the heart of enhanced collaboration is the ability to communicate effectively. Digital tools like instant messaging platforms, video conferencing software, and collaborative document editing services streamline communication by breaking down geographical barriers. Employees can connect with each other instantly, ensuring that vital information and ideas are shared without delay. This immediacy fosters a sense of closeness and real-time engagement that was previously unimaginable.

Consider Slack and Microsoft Teams, two platforms that have transformed how teams interact in real-time. By integrating chat, file sharing, and task management, these tools enable seamless communication and foster a collaborative culture. They provide a digital workspace where teams can brainstorm, resolve issues, and celebrate successes without leaving the platform. The informality and flexibility of these channels often encourage participation, as team members feel more at ease sharing ideas in a casual chat rather than formal settings.

Video conferencing has become a cornerstone of digital collaboration, particularly for remote or hybrid teams. Platforms like Zoom, Google Meet, and Webex offer face-to-face interaction without the need for physical presence. This visual connection is key to maintaining team morale and building trust. Seeing colleagues' expressions and body language can enhance understanding and empathy, which are critical in group dynamics. It also bridges cultural and linguistic gaps, providing a richer context to the spoken word.

However, the sheer proliferation of communication tools can lead to "communication overload," where team members feel inundated with constant notifications and messages. Balancing accessibility with the need for focused work periods is crucial to preventing burnout.

Teams must establish clear guidelines on tool use, specifying which platform to use for different types of communication. This clarity minimizes distractions and allows individuals to engage deeply when focused work is essential.

Another significant area where digital tools make a profound impact is project management. Platforms like Trello, Asana, and Monday.com have revolutionized how teams manage tasks and deadlines. These tools provide visibility into work progress, enabling team leaders to allocate resources effectively and identify potential bottlenecks promptly. Transparency in project management establishes accountability, motivating team members to track and fulfill their commitments.

Digital collaboration tools are not limited to communication and management. They also play a crucial role in fostering creativity and innovation. For instance, platforms like Miro and MURAL facilitate virtual whiteboarding sessions, enabling teams to brainstorm visually. These tools help capture and build on each other's ideas as if they were in the same room, expanding the team's creative capacity. The ability to iterate and collaborate on digital canvases transforms individual ideas into collective innovations.

Data analytics and AI-driven insights are also becoming indispensable components of digital collaboration. Tools that integrate these technologies provide teams with valuable insights by analyzing patterns in communication and project workflows. This can lead to data-informed decisions that optimize team performance. AI can also automate mundane tasks, freeing up time for employees to engage in more meaningful work that drives innovation.

Despite the immense potential of digital tools to enhance collaboration, one must not overlook the challenges they bring. Digital divides, such as varying levels of technological proficiency among team members, can impede effective tool utilization. Regular training and support can help bridge these gaps and ensure that all team members benefit equally from technological advancements. Moreover, fostering an inclusive team culture that embraces diverse technological abilities can empower individuals, building a resilient collaborative environment.

While technology offers new ways to collaborate, the relationship between humans and tools is inherently intertwined. A tool is only as effective as its implementation; hence, it is vital for teams to periodically assess the tools they use. Are they truly enhancing productivity, or merely adding complexity? Regular feedback loops and revisions to tool usage strategies ensure alignment with team goals and enhance the digital collaboration experience.

Furthermore, the emotional and psychological implications of digital interactions should not be underestimated. While virtual tools can replicate many aspects of physical presence, they can't entirely replace the warmth and subtleties of face-to-face interactions. To counteract potential feelings of isolation or disconnect, teams should incorporate activities that promote social bonding, such as virtual coffee breaks or collaborative games. These moments of levity strengthen team cohesion and ensure that technology serves as an enabler, not a barrier, to genuine connection.

Lastly, the adaptability of digital tools plays a pivotal role in their success. In a landscape where business needs change rapidly, the ability of tools to scale and integrate with other systems is paramount. Teams should prioritize tools that offer flexibility and customization, ensuring that they can evolve alongside organizational goals. This adaptability empowers teams to remain agile and responsive, characteristics that are indispensable in today's dynamic environment.

In conclusion, digital tools for enhanced collaboration are more than just utilities; they are catalysts for transformation in group interactions. They enable communication, streamline processes, and open avenues for innovation, all while posing challenges that require thoughtful management. The key to harnessing their full potential lies in understanding the unique needs of your team and crafting a balanced, inclusive approach to their implementation. When used effectively, digital tools not only enhance productivity but also enrich the human experiences that drive successful collaboration.

Navigating Technological Challenges

In our rapidly evolving digital landscape, technology undeniably shapes the very fabric of human interaction, particularly within groups. For anyone observing current group dynamics, it's impossible to ignore the pivotal role technology plays in both enhancing and complicating collaboration. As we dive into this section, it's essential to recognize that the digital revolution, while brimming with potential, also presents a unique set of challenges. To effectively navigate this terrain, we must be aware of both the obstacles and opportunities that accompany technological advancements.

One of the most significant challenges technology brings to group interactions is the risk of communication overload. In an era where information flows incessantly across various platforms, groups often grapple with the sheer volume of messages, data, and notifications. This can lead to cognitive overload, diminishing the quality of communication. Teams must develop strategies to filter and prioritize information to maintain focus and efficiency. Techniques like establishing clear communication protocols and integrating intelligent filtering systems can help manage this deluge.

Moreover, the reliance on digital communication tools can also lead to misunderstandings and misinterpretations. Without non-verbal cues, such as facial expressions and body language, messages can be misconstrued, potentially leading to conflict or confusion within a team. To counteract this, groups should emphasize clarity and brevity in their digital correspondence and leverage tools that incorporate video elements whenever possible.

Another aspect of technological challenges is the growing concern over privacy and security. As organizations increasingly depend on digital resources, protecting sensitive information becomes paramount. Breaches can undermine trust, both internally among team members and externally with clients and stakeholders. Teams should prioritize developing a robust cybersecurity strategy that includes regular training and updates on the latest security practices. Everyone involved must understand their role in safeguarding the team's digital environment.

Furthermore, the pace of technological change can leave teams feeling left behind if they aren't proactive in their approach to tech integration. It's crucial for groups to continuously educate themselves on emerging technologies relevant to their field. This doesn't mean everyone needs to become a tech expert, but fostering an environment of continuous learning and curiosity can help teams seamlessly adapt to new tools and methodologies. Encouraging a culture where questions are welcome and exploration is rewarded can significantly enhance a group's ability to integrate new technologies effectively.

Simultaneously, the challenge of ensuring equal access and opportunity arises. Not all individuals within a team may possess the same level of technological proficiency or access to technology, creating potential disparities. Ensuring that all team members have access to the necessary tools and training is vital for maintaining a cohesive and productive group dynamic. Initiatives such as regular training sessions, mentorship programs, and the provision of necessary hardware can bridge this gap and promote inclusivity.

On another front, the plethora of digital tools available today offers both opportunities and complications. Choosing the right tool for your group's needs can be overwhelming, yet it is critical for productivity and success. Teams should evaluate tools based on essential criteria such as usability, scalability, and integrations with other platforms they use. Aim for solutions that enhance collaboration without inducing additional complexity.

Despite these challenges, technology offers unparalleled opportunities for group interactions. Advanced collaborative tools enable teams to transcend geographical barriers, allowing for diverse and dynamic teams that bring a wealth of perspectives and ideas. Video conferencing platforms and real-time collaboration tools, for instance, facilitate seamless communication and innovative ideas, sparking creativity that might not materialize in a traditional setting.

Digital innovations also provide new ways to measure and improve team dynamics. Data analytics tools can yield insights into communication patterns, engagement levels, and overall team performance. By employing these technologies, leaders can make informed decisions to optimize team interactions and outcomes. Through regular analysis of such data, teams can identify areas for improvement and adjust strategies accordingly, leading to enhanced productivity and satisfaction.

In conclusion, while technology presents challenges to group interactions, it also offers remarkable opportunities to enhance collaboration if navigated thoughtfully. The key lies in leveraging technology to complement human interaction rather than replace it. By attuning to the nuanced needs of each team and continually adapting to technological shifts, groups can overcome potential roadblocks. With foresight and strategic planning, teams can harness the power of technology to achieve their collective goals and thrive in an ever-evolving digital landscape.

Chapter 14:
Building Effective
Collaborative Networks

In an interconnected world where no enterprise exists in isolation, building effective collaborative networks is not just beneficial, it's essential. The strength of a network lies in its ability to foster synergy, allowing teams to leverage diverse talents and insights to achieve common goals. At the heart of successful networks is a foundation of trust and open communication, where individuals can express their ideas without fear of judgment or exclusion. Just as a garden flourishes when nurtured, so do networks thrive with the right strategies and an understanding of each node's value. By cultivating relationships across various domains, individuals and teams can access a broader spectrum of resources, enhance innovation, and drive collective success. It's about creating a tapestry where each thread contributes to a larger picture, ensuring that the collaboration network remains agile and responsive to ever-evolving challenges and opportunities. Harnessing these networks effectively can turn any team into a powerhouse of creativity and productivity, paving the way for remarkable achievements.

The Importance of Collaboration Networks

In today's interconnected world, collaboration networks have become pivotal for unlocking the potential of collective endeavors. These networks, often complex and multifaceted, serve as the backbone of effective teamwork, facilitating the exchange of ideas and resources among individuals and groups. At their core, collaboration networks embody the essence of synergy — the concept that the collective effort of a group yields more substantial outcomes than the sum of individual efforts.

The importance of collaboration networks lies in their ability to foster innovation and creativity. When individuals are part of a well-connected network, they have enhanced access to diverse perspectives and knowledge bases. This diversity is instrumental in challenging conventional thinking, prompting members to explore novel solutions and creatively address problems. In environments that prize innovation, such as tech companies or creative agencies, these networks are not merely beneficial but essential for maintaining a competitive edge.

Moreover, collaboration networks often facilitate quicker decision-making processes. In traditional hierarchical settings, decisions can become bottlenecked, stalled by layers of approval and bureaucracy. Networks, on the other hand, enable flatter and more agile structures where information flows more freely. This setup allows teams to be more responsive and adaptive, addressing challenges swiftly and efficiently as they arise. The flexibility offered by effective networks is particularly advantageous in fast-evolving industries where the pace of change requires nimble management.

On a motivational level, being part of a collaborative network can significantly impact individual and group morale. Networks that promote collaboration often foster a sense of belonging and shared purpose. When individuals feel connected to their peers and see themselves as integral components of the group's success, they are more likely to be motivated and engaged in their work. This collective identity and sense of purpose fuel perseverance, even in the face of setbacks.

Furthermore, collaboration networks can play a critical role in personal and professional growth. As members engage with the network, they can develop new skills, learn from mentors, and gain insights into different fields and industries. This continuous learning enriches individuals' professional journeys, laying the groundwork for innovation. Organizations that cultivate such networks not only benefit from a more skilled and knowledgeable workforce but also from enhanced employee satisfaction and retention.

Interpersonal relationships are also strengthened within collaboration networks. The continuous interaction among members builds trust and mutual respect, which are critical for effective collaboration. Trust is a vital currency in networked settings, as it underpins open communication, risk-taking, and cooperative problem-solving. In environments where trust thrives, individuals feel comfortable sharing ideas, even those that are undeveloped or unconventional. This openness often leads to breakthroughs and innovations that would be impossible in more isolated or distrustful settings.

Despite these benefits, maintaining an effective collaboration network isn't without its challenges. As networks grow in size and complexity, they can become difficult to manage, and the risk of information overload becomes prevalent. However, with strategic structuring and the adoption of clear communication channels, these challenges can be mitigated. Emphasizing quality over quantity in relationships within the network can ensure that the channels remain effective rather than overwhelming.

In essence, collaboration networks transform the way teams and organizations operate. They bring together diverse talents and perspectives, fostering an environment ripe for creativity and innovation. These networks also streamline processes, enhance motivation, support personal and professional development, and strengthen the relational fabric of teams. As we move forward in an increasingly complex and interconnected world, the importance of cultivating and maintaining robust collaboration networks cannot be understated. They are not just strategies for organizational success but building blocks for progress and development in any field. Only through effective collaboration can we hope to face and overcome the multifaceted challenges of the future.

Strategies for Network Building

Network building is an essential strategy for creating collaborative environments that maximize potential and foster innovation. As organizations become increasingly complex and interconnected, the need for effective networks becomes undeniable. Building these networks is not just about connecting individuals—it's about weaving a web of trust, shared values, and common goals that can carry teams through challenges and propel them toward collective success.

The process starts with identifying key stakeholders who will form the backbone of the network. These individuals don't have to be in leadership positions, but they should possess influence and a knack for fostering relationships. Identifying and involving these key players who are inspired by a shared vision can ignite the network's momentum. Once identified, it's essential to ensure that their goals align with the network's overarching objectives. This alignment creates a shared foundation upon which the network can be built, promoting a cohesive and united effort.

To nurture these connections, open communication channels must be established. This involves creating forums—both digital and face-to-face—where ideas can be freely exchanged. Encouraging dialogue not only stimulates intellectual diversity, which is critical for innovation, but also deepens mutual understanding. It's through this continuous exchange of ideas that strong bonds form. The friction from different viewpoints can also spark creative problem-solving, enabling the network to refine its strategies and achieve higher levels of performance.

Another crucial strategy is fostering a culture of collaboration. This means prioritizing cooperative endeavors over competitive ones and celebrating synergies that arise from collective efforts. Building a network rooted in collaboration requires an environment where team members feel psychologically safe to express ideas without fear of judgment. By establishing norms of respect and inclusion, members of the network can operate without the barriers of hierarchy or departmental silos, which often inhibit creativity and flow.

Networks thrive on trust, and trustworthiness should be modeled at every opportunity. Trust is cultivated through consistency, transparency, and empathy. When network members can depend on each other to follow through on commitments, communicate candidly, and understand each other's perspectives, trust flourishes. In return, this trust underpins efforts to achieve common goals and is a critical component of a network that can weather setbacks and foster resilience in the face of challenges.

Leverage technology to build and maintain these networks effectively. Use digital tools like collaborative platforms, social media, and project management software that bridge geographical and functional divides. These technologies can enhance connectivity, providing real-time interaction and information sharing. However, it's also crucial to recognize and address the potential pitfalls, such as digital fatigue and information overload, ensuring that these tools genuinely foster—rather than hinder—interaction and productivity.

Recognizing the importance of diversity and inclusion within networks can't be overstated. Bringing together a diverse group of people does more than just reflect social responsibility—it enhances creativity and broadens perspectives within the network. Diverse networks are better equipped to solve problems innovatively because they draw from a wider range of experiences and viewpoints. Implement strategies that actively seek diverse voices and foster an inclusive atmosphere where everyone feels valued and heard. This approach not only strengthens the network but also enriches the quality of its output.

Empowerment is another pillar of effective network building. Encourage members to take initiative and assume leadership roles in line with their expertise and interests. When individuals are empowered, they're more likely to contribute their best efforts and engage deeply with the network's goals. Empowerment also involves granting autonomy where possible, allowing network members the freedom to explore creative solutions and experiments without being tethered by unnecessary constraints.

Monitor and measure the network's progress and impact regularly. Utilize metrics to evaluate the effectiveness of interactions, the quality of relationships, and the achievement of goals. However, these metrics shouldn't focus solely on outputs—consider the process, too. Are the methods used fostering collaboration? Is there a persistent culture of learning and adaptation within the network? Reflecting on these questions can provide valuable insights into areas for improvement.

A successful strategy for network building must include a commitment to continuous learning and adaptation. Networks should remain nimble and open to change, prepared to pivot when necessary. Organize regular reviews to reflect on successes and failures, encouraging an environment of learning from experiences rather than stigmatizing mistakes. This mindset not only strengthens the network's adaptability but also ensures it remains relevant and effective amidst changing landscapes.

Ultimately, building effective collaborative networks is a dynamic and ongoing process. It requires intentionality in fostering relationships based on trust, collaboration, and mutual respect. Strategies thoughtfully implemented build a robust framework for innovation, resilience, and collective achievement. As networks mature, they generate their own momentum, continually enhancing the group's potential to achieve greater heights.

Chapter 15:
Groupthink and Its Effects

In the complex realm of group dynamics, groupthink emerges as a formidable force that can subtly derail decision-making and stifle innovation. This psychological phenomenon occurs when the desire for harmony or cohesion within a group leads members to prioritize consensus over critical thinking or diverse opinions. The effects of groupthink can be far-reaching, resulting in poor decisions, missed opportunities, and in some cases, catastrophic outcomes. The unchecked momentum of groupthink pressures individuals to conform, often overriding personal convictions in favor of unanimity. Yet, understanding its telltale signs—such as the suppression of dissent and an illusion of invulnerability—can empower leaders and teams to counteract its effects. Employing strategies like encouraging open dialogue, appointing a devil's advocate, and fostering an environment where questioning is welcomed are crucial in safeguarding groups from the pitfalls of groupthink. By championing a culture of openness and critical evaluation, teams not only fortify their decision-making processes but also harness the creative potential that diverse perspectives bring.

Identifying Signs of Groupthink

In the realm of group dynamics, the concept of groupthink can subtly weave its way into the fabric of decision-making processes. It's a psychological phenomenon where the desire for harmony or conformity within a group leads to irrational or dysfunctional outcomes. Understanding and identifying signs of groupthink are paramount for anyone looking to harness the power of effective teamwork and collaborative decision-making.

One of the classic hallmarks of groupthink is an illusion of invulnerability. This manifests when a group develops a shared belief that it cannot fail, leading members to take excessive risks or overlook potential pitfalls. For instance, a project team might neglect thorough market analysis, convinced that their innovative product is a guaranteed success. This misplaced belief can spell disaster when reality doesn't align with expectations.

Another core indicator of groupthink is collective rationalization. Members of a group often dismiss warnings or contradictory viewpoints to preserve group consensus. This denial of reality can be subtle yet pervasive, manifesting as group members providing illogical justifications for past failures or overlooking current warning signs.

Staring down the barrel of a collective rationalization requires a mindful awareness of the group's narrative. Is the feedback being dismissed too quickly? Are alternative viewpoints being sidelined merely because they disrupt the apparent group harmony? It's critical to foster an environment where differing opinions are encouraged and valued, as they can often be the most insightful.

Moreover, the presence of self-censorship among group members serves as a crucial warning sign. Individuals may hesitate to express dissenting opinions due to fear of disrupting group equilibrium. Such self-imposed silence stifles creativity and innovation, as team members second-guess their contributions. Encouraging open dialogue and assuring team members that their opinions are valued can mitigate this tendency.

A further symptom is the emergence of stereotyped views of outsiders. Groups entrenched in groupthink often develop an "us versus them" mentality. They may demonize or underestimate rival groups or individuals, disregarding their potential contributions or competitive advantages.

This stereotyping restricts the flow of creative ideas and solutions. By actively seeking external input and fostering collaborations across different teams or organizations, groups can break free from this isolated mindset, enriching their perspectives with diverse input.

Additionally, a sense of unquestioned morality often accompanies groupthink. Members perceive their decisions as morally superior, leading them to make unethical choices without thorough examination of the implications. It's crucial for teams to maintain ethical standards and consider the wider impact of their decisions.

Direct pressure on dissenters is another red flag. When individuals who voice dissent are met with hostility or pressure to conform, it stifles genuine debate and critical analysis. This peer pressure ensures conformity, but at the expense of potentially game-changing insights.

To combat this, it's vital to create a team culture where questioning is not just tolerated but actively encouraged. Leaders can play a significant role by inviting criticism and demonstrating receptiveness to diverse viewpoints.

Similarly, the presence of mindguards in a group can hinder open communication. Mindguards act as self-appointed protectors of the group, shielding it from dissenting opinions and filtering information that threatens consensus. This dynamic can insulate a group from valuable external feedback, compounding the risks of groupthink.

Recognizing the role of mindguards and dismantling this protective barrier is essential for maintaining transparency.

Establishing clear channels for information flow and encouraging direct communication can minimize this threat.

Finally, an often-overlooked symptom is the illusion of unanimity. The silence or inaction of some group members is misconstrued as agreement, leading to a false sense of consensus. This dynamic can derail the decision-making process, as critical voices remain unheard and unconsidered.

Effective team leaders must be adept at reading between the lines, ensuring that all team members feel empowered to voice their opinions. Structured feedback sessions and anonymous input mechanisms can help reveal hidden dissent and facilitate a more complete understanding of group sentiment.

Identifying signs of groupthink is not just about spotting weaknesses, but about fostering an environment where critical thought thrives. By consciously cultivating a culture that values diverse opinions and constructive criticism, teams can avoid the pitfalls of groupthink and engage in more informed and balanced decision-making processes.

In this light, the resilience of a group lies not in its ability to avoid conflicts, but in its capacity to welcome and resolve them through healthy discourse. Encouraging a diverse array of perspectives while remaining vigilant for signs of conformity paves the way for innovative solutions and sustainable success.

Understanding these dynamics empowers leaders and team members alike to navigate the intricate landscape of group behavior, minimizing the risks of groupthink while enhancing collective performance. At its core, identifying and addressing these signs is part of a broader commitment to cultivating dynamic, agile, and forward-thinking teams.

Strategies to Prevent Groupthink

In the complex tapestry of group interactions, groupthink emerges as a silent adversary, imperceptibly weaving threads of conformity into the fabric of decision-making. Recognizing and countering this phenomenon isn't just an academic exercise; it is a pragmatic necessity for effective teamwork and leadership. This section focuses on unraveling the elements that foster groupthink, followed by actionable strategies to mitigate its pervasive effects.

One foundational approach to preventing groupthink is cultivating an environment that values genuine diversity of thought. Teams often fall prey to groupthink when members feel compelled to conform to dominant views, stifling creativity and critical analysis. Encouraging diverse perspectives can break this cycle, fostering a culture where dissent and dialogue are not only accepted but encouraged. It's essential for leaders to model this behavior, showing that questioning the status quo is a pathway to innovation, not a threat to cohesion.

Leadership plays a pivotal role in curbing groupthink. Effective leaders understand the delicate balance between guiding a team and overpowering it with their own ideas. By championing an open-door policy and actively soliciting input from all team members, leaders can create a safe space where different viewpoints can surface without the fear of reprisal or ostracism. Regularly rotating leadership roles within a team can also democratize decision-making, offering fresh insights and reducing the hierarchical pressures that often stifle honest discourse.

Another critical strategy involves enhancing decision-making processes with structured methodologies that challenge the group's assumptions. Techniques such as the Delphi method or devil's advocacy are powerful tools. The Delphi method, for instance, involves rounds of anonymous input, preventing dominance by more vocal members and minimizing perceived pressure to conform. Similarly, appointing a devil's advocate can stimulate healthy debate, ensuring that all aspects of a decision are rigorously examined before a consensus is reached.

Effective communication is crucial in the fight against groupthink. Teams should be trained to recognize and articulate when they feel their voice is being overshadowed. This awareness begins with nurturing emotional intelligence within the group. Emotionally intelligent teams are more adept at managing conflicts and voicing concerns constructively, making them resilient against the allure of uniformity. Furthermore, structured feedback sessions can help surface underlying issues, fostering transparency and continuous improvement in how the team communicates.

The physical and psychological spaces where teams convene also impact the likelihood of groupthink. Virtual settings, while convenient, can obscure non-verbal cues and lead to misunderstandings. Teams should prioritize regular in-person meetings or video calls, where body language can add valuable context to verbal communication. Even the layout of a meeting room can influence dynamics—circular seating arrangements, for example, promote equality and openness, subtly discouraging the formation of subgroups or echo chambers.

Building a culture of reflective practice can also serve as a bulwark against groupthink. After every major decision or project, hosting debriefing sessions where teams analyze what worked and what didn't can surface hidden assumptions and biases. These sessions should not be perfunctory critiques but constructive dialogues aimed at fostering learning. Reflective practice encourages members to become self-aware and metacognitive, continuously assessing and adjusting their thinking patterns.

It's essential to establish clear but flexible guidelines for decision-making. A rigid adherence to rules can inadvertently stifle innovation, while a total lack of structure can lead to chaos. Balance is key. Teams should experiment with various decision-making frameworks, like consensus-building or majority votes, tailoring them to the specific context and objectives of the team. This adaptability ensures that the process remains dynamic and responsive to the group's evolving needs.

Inter-disciplinary collaboration offers another valuable perspective. Engaging with individuals outside of the core team can provide fresh insights and disrupt entrenched patterns of thought. For instance, inviting external experts or stakeholders to contribute at key stages of a project can illuminate blind spots and challenge prevailing assumptions. This cross-pollination of ideas not only enhances creativity but also fortifies the team against groupthink.

Finally, fostering a mindset of continuous learning and growth within the team can act as an antidote to the complacency that often breeds groupthink. This involves not only formal training sessions but also encouraging team members to pursue personal development activities. When individuals are consistently exposed to new ideas and ways of thinking, they are more likely to bring that innovative spirit back to the group. Learning doesn't stop at acquiring knowledge; it involves questioning existing paradigms and relentlessly seeking improvement.

The true power of effective group dynamics lies in harnessing the vast potential of diverse ideas while steering clear of the pitfalls that collective decision-making can entail. By implementing strategies to prevent groupthink, teams are empowered to make sound decisions that reflect a true amalgamation of their collective wisdom. Each member's voice enriches the group, and through these robust interactions, the team can transform challenges into opportunities for innovation and excellence. In the end, the measure of a team's success isn't just in avoiding failure but in creating a culture where every decision is a stepping stone to greater heights.

Chapter 16:
Teams in Crisis Situations

In times of crisis, the resilience and adaptability of teams are put to the test, demanding rapid responses and decisive leadership to steer through tumultuous waters. During such pivotal moments, leaders must step up, not just as decision-makers, but as anchors of stability, guiding their teams with clarity and empathy. Team cohesion can become fragile, yet it's precisely in these challenging times that a shared mission can unite members, fostering solidarity and collective resilience. By leveraging established trust and open communication channels, teams can navigate uncertainty, turning challenges into opportunities for growth and innovation. As individuals come together to support one another, acknowledging each person's unique contributions, they form a cohesive unit, capable of withstanding pressures that could otherwise fracture unprepared groups. Ultimately, facing crises head-on often reveals untapped potential within teams, setting the stage for transformation and strengthening the bonds that define true teamwork.

Leadership During Crisis

In the face of a crisis, leadership isn't just important; it's imperative. The ability to guide a team through tumultuous times requires a unique blend of steadiness, empathy, and decisiveness. During crises, leaders must first acknowledge the gravity of the situation, setting a tone that is neither alarmist nor dismissive. Acknowledgment establishes trust, signaling to the team that their leader is aware and actively engaged in navigating the uncertainty.

Crisis leadership often begins with effective communication. This means clearly articulating the current situation, potential implications, and the steps being taken to address the issue. Ambiguity can fuel fear and speculation, which can cripple a team. A leader must communicate with transparency and consistency, ensuring that all team members receive the information they need to perform effectively. This includes not only conveying facts but also projecting a sense of calm assurance that the situation is under control, which can provide a psychological anchor for the team.

Yet, great crisis leaders do more than just communicate. They listen. In practice, this means creating open channels for team members to express concerns, offer insights, and provide feedback. Active listening demonstrates respect for diverse perspectives and can often unearth innovative solutions to complex problems. This participatory approach can also help to maintain morale by involving team members in the problem-solving process, reinforcing their value within the team.

Another critical aspect of crisis leadership is adaptability. Circumstances can change rapidly during a crisis, requiring leaders to be flexible in their strategies. While having a plan is essential, the ability to pivot and adjust that plan in response to new information or unforeseen challenges is equally vital. This adaptability shows the team that the leader is responsive to real-world dynamics, rather than rigidly adhering to a preconceived strategy that may no longer be viable.

Moreover, it's crucial for leaders to demonstrate resilience. Crises can be exhausting, both mentally and physically, and leaders must model strength and endurance for their teams. This doesn't mean that leaders should disregard their own limitations, but rather that they should acknowledge setbacks and bounce back from them, showing a commitment to moving forward despite difficulties.

Empathy is another cornerstone of effective leadership during crisis. Leaders should recognize that each team member may react differently to stress and uncertainty. Some may become withdrawn, others might channel their anxiety into hyper-productivity, and still others may need additional support to manage their emotions. By recognizing these varied responses and providing appropriate support, leaders can help maintain a cohesive and supportive team environment.

At times, crisis leadership involves making tough decisions. These decisions often require a delicate balance between quick action and thoughtful consideration. Relying on a mixture of data-driven analysis and intuitive judgment, leaders must weigh the potential impact of their choices. It is a delicate dance between speed and deliberation, where the stakes are high and the pressure to act decisively is ever-present.

Delegation also plays a significant role during crises. Leaders can become bottlenecks if they try to handle everything themselves. Effective delegation not only alleviates pressure from the leader but also empowers team members by entrusting them with significant responsibilities. This can stimulate engagement and foster a sense of ownership and autonomy among team members.

Finally, reflecting on the crisis once it's over is a crucial step. Leaders should facilitate a debrief with the team, discussing what strategies worked, which decisions faltered, and how the team can improve moving forward. This reflection helps to reinforce lessons learned and can prepare the team for future challenges, turning crises into valuable learning experiences.

In summary, leadership during a crisis demands a blend of empathy, communication, adaptability, and resilience. By leveraging these qualities, leaders can not only steer their teams through immediate difficulties but also cultivate a stronger, more cohesive unit ready to face future challenges head-on.

Maintaining Team Cohesion

Maintaining team cohesion during crisis situations is both an art and a science. Crisis situations often inject a level of unpredictability and stress that can test even the most resilient teams. Amidst the chaos, the glue that holds a team together is its collective sense of identity and purpose. When the stakes are high, the importance of having a vision that everyone can buy into becomes undeniable. It fosters a unity that goes beyond individual roles and responsibilities, creating a shared narrative of resilience and determination. This shared mission can be the keystone in maintaining cohesion.

At the heart of team cohesion during crises is trust. It's not just about believing that your teammates will do their jobs; it's also about trusting that they'll have your back when things go south. This level of trust is cultivated through transparency and communication. Teams need leaders who communicate openly about the challenges at hand without sugarcoating the reality yet inspire confidence that they're equipped to navigate through it. Clear, honest communication prevents misunderstandings and keeps the team aligned.

In times of crisis, emotions run high. Recognizing and addressing these emotions is critical. When stress peaks, it can lead to fragmented relationships and a breakdown in communication. Facilitating an environment where team members feel heard and valued is essential. Here, emotional intelligence plays a pivotal role. Teams need individuals who can empathize with others, rapidly adapt to different personality types, and foster a culture of support. This kindness leads to solidarity and helps weather the storm together.

Flexibility and adaptability are key attributes for cohesive teams in crises. Conditions may change rapidly, and hanging onto old ways of working can be detrimental. A flexible team finds strength in its ability to pivot and approach problems from different angles. This might require redefining roles to match current needs, thereby allowing each member to contribute their specialties in shifting circumstances. The ability to adapt while maintaining a shared goal creates a dynamic team that can thrive despite adversity.

Moreover, a strong focus on small wins can keep morale high. Celebrating minor victories reminds the team that progress is being made, even if the overall situation seems daunting. These celebrations provide a necessary boost of motivation and reinforce the team's unity. Consistently recognizing effort and dedication also strengthens camaraderie and emboldens team members to push forward.

Teams in crisis can benefit greatly from established rituals and routines. Although it might seem counterintuitive, routines provide a sense of normalcy and stability in unpredictable situations. Whether it's through regular check-ins or a shared debriefing session to reflect on the day's achievements and challenges, such rituals ground the team, offering a moment of solace and cohesion amidst the whirlwind.

Building psychological safety is equally crucial. Members should feel comfortable expressing dissenting opinions or raising potential concerns without fear of retribution. This openness is vital because it assures team members that their insights are valued, preventing groupthink and encouraging innovative solutions. Creating a safe space where vulnerability is embraced can transform individual courage into collective action.

Importantly, leaders must serve as role models in maintaining cohesion. They set the tone for interaction, collaboration, and resilience. By demonstrating calmness, empathy, and a steadfast commitment to the team's welfare, leaders inspire the same qualities in others. Their ability to navigate the crisis with a composed demeanor provides a reassuring presence that grounds the team.

Finally, a profound sense of intentionality underlines successful cohesive efforts. When teams unite under an authentic purpose, every action, discussion, and decision is infused with meaning. Team cohesion in crises isn't merely about staying together—it's about moving forward with a shared understanding that goes beyond the immediate crisis, propelling the team towards a brighter, collective future.

In essence, crisis situations test the mettle of teams like no other conditions. Cohesion doesn't happen by accident but through deliberate efforts to build trust, clear communication, emotional acknowledgment, adaptability, and leadership. When teams harness these elements, they're not just surviving the crisis— they're strengthening their bonds and emerging more unified and resilient.

Chapter 17:
Negotiation and Persuasion in Groups

In the complex world of group dynamics, mastering the art of negotiation and persuasion is essential for fostering cooperation and driving effective collaboration. These skills aren't just about convincing others to your point of view; they're about crafting environments where ideas can thrive and mutual respect prevails. To negotiate successfully within groups, it's vital to understand the interests and motivations of each member. Effective negotiation hinges on active listening, patience, and finding common ground where all parties feel valued. Similarly, persuasion in groups requires more than eloquent arguments — it involves building trust, demonstrating empathy, and effectively harnessing emotional intelligence. When team members can persuasively present their perspectives while remaining open to others' ideas, innovation and progress flourish. Thus, at the heart of successful negotiation and persuasion lies a commitment to the group's collective goals, ensuring that the path forward is paved with shared understanding and mutual benefit.

Effective Negotiation Techniques

Negotiation within groups is a dynamic art shaped by the multifaceted human elements of each participant. At the heart of effective negotiation lies the understanding that each group member brings a unique set of perspectives, priorities, and emotions to the table. Crafting successful negotiation strategies hinges on balancing these individual differences while fostering a collective sense of purpose and collaboration.

The start of any negotiation process is all about preparation. Successful negotiators invest time understanding not just their objectives but also the priorities and possible objections of fellow group members. This involves gathering information, anticipating questions, and preparing evidence to support your stance. However, the preparation doesn't stop there. They must remain flexible, adapting to how the conversation shifts and evolves. This dual focus on planning and adaptability is crucial in creating persuasive and effective dialogue in group settings.

Building rapport is another cornerstone of effective negotiation. Establishing trust and understanding among group members paves the way for smoother interactions. Creating a friendly and open environment encourages participants to be more forthcoming with their thoughts and ideas. Simple gestures such as active listening, acknowledging others' contributions, and showing empathy can significantly enhance the negotiation process.

Active listening, in particular, cannot be overstated. It's more than just hearing words; it's about understanding emotion and intent. By actively listening, negotiators can pick up on unspoken concerns or reservations, allowing them to address these aspects explicitly. This not only helps in steering the discussion constructively but also assures other members that their inputs are valued.

Once a foundation of trust and understanding is formed, employing a collaborative negotiation style can further augment effectiveness. This style focuses on finding a middle ground where all group members feel they have had a fair say in the outcome. It's about transforming potential divisiveness into opportunities for consensus and compromise, ensuring that solutions benefit the group collectively rather than favoring a single viewpoint.

Handling conflicts within negotiations often becomes inevitable. This requires negotiators to be skilled at conflict resolution techniques that reduce tension and promote understanding. Strategies such as reframing contentious issues, exploring underlying interests, and focusing on mutual goals help negotiators move past impasses, turning confrontation into cooperation.

The capacity to influence, without appearing domineering, is also vital. Drawing on social proof and establishing authority appropriately can make a difference here. While demonstrating expertise and credibility is important, it's equally crucial to encourage participation and acknowledge diverse perspectives. This balance shows respect for group diversity, and leverages the additive power of varied voices in forming a coherent group consensus.

Emotion management plays another significant role in negotiation. Emotions, both our own and others', can drive or derail the negotiation process. Acknowledging emotions transparently and understanding their impact helps negotiators maintain a level of professionalism and focus within the group. Techniques such as mindfulness and emotional regulation can be instrumental in managing heated dialogues, ensuring they remain productive rather than destructive.

When dealing with more complex issues or larger groups, the use of structured frameworks can prove beneficial. Tools like BATNA (Best Alternative to a Negotiated Agreement) give negotiators clear benchmarks and fallback options, enhancing their confidence during discussions. Additionally, structured dialogues such as interest-based negotiation encourage group members to explore beyond fixed positions, uncovering the interests that underpin their demands.

Visual aids can also significantly enhance negotiation outcomes. Charts, graphs, and data points provide concrete support for arguments, draw attention away from emotional disputes, and ground discussions in fact. They help visualize potential solutions and outcomes, making abstract concepts more tangible for the group.

The timing in negotiations is another tactical consideration. The tempo of discussions can influence outcomes, whether it's allowing pause to reflect and reassess or maintaining momentum to press toward conclusion. At times, a well-placed question or strategic silence can be more effective than persistent argumentation.

It's also essential for negotiators to reflect on the negotiation process immediately after it concludes. Evaluating what strategies worked, what didn't, and how group dynamics played out helps refine skills for future interactions. This habit of continuous improvement ensures negotiators remain adaptable, learning from each experience to become more effective collaborators.

Finally, it's worth recognizing that every group negotiation is a unique opportunity. The techniques discussed offer a guide but must be customized to fit the specific context of each negotiation. By doing so, negotiators can build stronger, more productive group interactions that harness the collective potential of diverse participants.

Persuasion Strategies for Groups

Persuasion in group settings isn't just about convincing others of a particular viewpoint; it's about shifting the entire group's perspective in a way that aligns with a shared goal or vision. This transformation relies on understanding group dynamics deeply. The synergy found in collective decision-making can be a powerful catalyst for effective persuasion. It's not merely the sharpening of rhetoric but the strategic enhancement of collective reasoning that drives successful persuasion among groups.

To embark on this journey, one must first recognize the importance of context. Why is the group assembled? What are the shared interests or goals that can be leveraged? Establishing this context creates a conducive environment where group members can engage openly, contributing to a more persuasive impact. By understanding the unspoken rules of a group's culture, persuasive efforts can be aligned to amplify resonance and receptiveness.

At the core of any persuasive strategy lies trust and credibility. Without these elements, even the most logical arguments may fall on deaf ears. Establishing trust begins with demonstrating authenticity and transparency, allowing group members to see the genuine intent behind the persuasion. By sharing relevant personal experience and expertise, persuaders can enhance their credibility, making group members more inclined to align with the proposed ideas.

In groups, persuasion often requires the skillful use of influence rather than direct control. The artful application of social proof, where individuals are more inclined to adopt ideas that are believed or practiced by others in their group, illustrates this concept. When individuals observe that others in their circle are supportive of an idea, they are more susceptible to being persuaded themselves. Strategically demonstrating early adopters or influencers within the group can help in swaying the opinions of others.

Emotional intelligence plays a significant role in persuasion. Recognizing and empathizing with the emotions of group members allows for tailored messaging that resonates on a personal level. This empathetic approach can transform potential resistance into acceptance, as individuals feel understood and valued. Aligning persuasive efforts with the emotional landscape of the group nurtures a genuine connection that rational arguments alone may not achieve.

To further enhance persuasive efforts, it is crucial to listen actively. Active listening fosters an environment where individuals feel heard and respected, prompting them to reciprocate with openness. It also provides the persuader with valuable insights into the concerns and motivations of group members, enabling the crafting of arguments that directly address these areas.

Finding alignment within the group's goals can also bolster persuasion. Establishing a common ground or a shared vision helps unify the group's efforts toward a single objective. Highlighting benefits that align with group values or addressing group-specific challenges in the proposal can effectively pivot the group's mindset in favor of the intended outcome. In doing so, persuasion becomes not an external imposition, but an internal evolution.

Timing also plays a critical role in persuasion. Understanding when the group is most receptive, whether it's at the start of a meeting before fatigue sets in, or during a moment of collective success and goodwill, can dramatically enhance the effectiveness of persuasive interactions. Strategically timing engagements allows persuaders to capitalize on windows of opportunity where group members are more primed for influence.

Visual and narrative storytelling is another powerful tool. Stories connect with people on a deeper level, addressing not only the intellect but also emotions. Narratives that include relatable characters or scenarios can convey complex ideas in a memorable and impactful way. Likewise, visuals can simplify and synthesize information, allowing group members to grasp and retain messages more effectively than through words alone.

When faced with diverse opinions, consensus-building offers a pathway toward persuasion. Incorporating an open forum for discussion where all members can contribute ideas enhances collective buy-in. Offering compromise solutions or hybrid models that integrate diverse perspectives can foster a collaborative environment where group members feel their input is valued and thus more likely to support the outcome.

Acknowledging and addressing counterarguments openly is an additional strategy for strengthening persuasion. By proactively discussing potential drawbacks or opposing views, persuaders demonstrate their comprehensive understanding of the issue. This honesty builds trust and showcases analytical integrity, making group members more likely to consider the main argument favorably.

Lastly, embodying the change you wish to see in the group sets a persuasive precedent. When group members observe the positive impact of the proposed ideas in action, it can inspire them to follow suit. This modeling of behavior engenders respect and demonstrates the feasibility and benefits of adopting such changes, ultimately facilitating a smoother transition in group opinion.

In summary, successful persuasion in groups involves a nuanced blend of understanding group dynamics, building trust, and emotionally intelligent communication. By strategically applying these components, persuasion becomes an artful yet intentional process, fostering cooperation and alignment within the group. As we continue to explore the multifaceted nature of group influence, these strategies provide a practical foundation to navigate the complexities of communal persuasion effectively.

Chapter 18:
Ethical Considerations
in Group Dynamics

In the intricate dance of group dynamics, ethical considerations often serve as the guiding light, defining the boundaries of acceptable behavior and shaping the moral fabric of team interactions. The complexities of working within groups can sometimes lead to ethical challenges, such as conflicts of interest, power imbalances, and the potential for groupthink to overshadow individual moral judgment. It's imperative for teams to develop clear ethical guidelines that not only emphasize transparency and fairness but also foster an environment where every voice is heard and respected. By embedding ethics at the core of group operations, leaders and team members can ensure decisions and actions align with shared values and societal norms. This ethical consciousness not only strengthens trust within teams but also enhances their reputation in the broader community, paving the way for sustainable success and harmony. Balancing individual interests with collective goals requires mindfulness and, often, courageous conversations that challenge the status quo, thus propelling teams toward a more ethical and effective way of achieving their objectives.

Ethical Challenges in Group Settings

In today's interconnected world, the dynamics within groups have become increasingly complex, posing unique ethical challenges that demand attention and thoughtful navigation. These challenges often emerge as the interests, values, and cultures of individual members intersect and sometimes clash. Understanding and addressing these ethical dilemmas are essential for cultivating environments where trust, transparency, and integrity can flourish.

One of the foremost ethical challenges in group settings is the issue of confidentiality. When group members share sensitive information—whether in business negotiations, therapy groups, or team projects—preserving the confidentiality of these disclosures is paramount. Breaches of confidentiality can result in a loss of trust, legal implications, and reputational damage. Therefore, setting clear guidelines and expectations around the handling of private information remains vital.

Bias and discrimination represent another significant ethical obstacle in group settings. Groups can sometimes amplify individual biases, leading to discriminatory practices that exclude certain members based on race, gender, age, or other characteristics. Bias can manifest subtly through microaggressions or overtly through exclusion from opportunities. To counteract this, groups must actively foster inclusion and equity, creating an environment where diverse perspectives are welcomed and valued.

The power dynamics within a group can lead to ethical dilemmas as well. Unequal distribution of power may result in coercion, where dominant members impose their views or decisions on others. This can suppress dissenting voices and stifle creativity. Ethical leadership should encourage an open dialogue where all members have an opportunity to contribute and influence outcomes, ensuring that the power dynamics do not overrule fairness and collaboration.

Groupthink is a phenomenon that poses ethical risks by compromising critical thinking and individuality for the sake of consensus. When group's unanimity is pursued at the expense of rational decision-making, it can lead to unethical outcomes. Members may feel pressured to conform, ignoring potential moral or practical objections. Cultivating a culture that values diverse viewpoints and rigorous questioning is key to mitigating the risks of groupthink.

Conflicts of interest within groups can also introduce ethical complications, particularly in professional settings. When individuals prioritize personal gain over the group's objectives, it can lead to competing loyalties and raise ethical concerns. Establishing clear, transparent policies that address potential conflicts of interest can help maintain the group's integrity and focus on shared goals.

Similarly, accountability and responsibility are crucial ethical considerations. In group projects or team efforts, determining who is responsible for certain outcomes can become blurred. Members may attribute failures to the collective, thereby evading personal accountability. Cultivating a culture of ownership, where each member understands their individual contributions and responsibilities, can mitigate these issues, leading to more honest and productive group interactions.

Moreover, the rapid pace of technology brings additional ethical challenges to group dynamics. With digital communication tools, maintaining respectful, ethical interactions across online platforms becomes increasingly significant. Cyberbullying, data privacy concerns, and digital misconduct are new challenges that need to be tackled with robust ethical guidelines and education in the use of technology.

The ethical dimensions of decision-making processes in groups also present complex challenges. Decisions made through voting, consensus, or delegation each have inherent ethical implications. Choosing a decision-making process that aligns with the group's values and ethical considerations is crucial to ensuring fairness and justice.

Finally, ethical challenges can arise from the need to balance group loyalty with outside obligations. Members may struggle when their commitments to the group conflict with their duties to external stakeholders, such as families, communities, or professional bodies. Developing ethical guidelines that respect both the internal group dynamics and external responsibilities can help members navigate these situations more effectively.

In conclusion, ethical challenges in group settings are deeply intertwined with the very fabric of group life, affecting trust, decision-making, and collaboration. By acknowledging these challenges and intentionally working to address them, groups can create ethical standards that underpin their interactions and enhance their collective behavior. This proactive approach not only resolves ethical dilemmas but also strengthens the group's overall effectiveness and cohesion.

Developing Ethical Guidelines

In the intricate tapestry of group dynamics, the ethical component is a thread that must be woven with care and precision. As individuals come together to form teams, they invariably bring a diverse array of values and principles. This diversity is a strength but also necessitates a coherent framework to guide behavior and decisions within the group. The formation of ethical guidelines becomes not only a practical necessity but a moral imperative to ensure that collective actions reflect shared human values.

At the heart of developing ethical guidelines is the acknowledgment that ethics in group settings is not monolithic. Different groups will encounter unique challenges and dilemmas that require tailored approaches. The first step in this process is to conduct a thorough assessment of the group's nature, purpose, and composition. For instance, a corporate team focused on innovation will have different ethical considerations than a non-profit organization dedicated to humanitarian efforts. Identifying these nuances is crucial in shaping guidelines that resonate with the specific needs and goals of the group.

Once the foundation is laid, engaging all members in the development process is essential. This inclusivity ensures that the guidelines are not only representative of the collective but also fosters a sense of ownership and commitment among members. When individuals feel that their voices have been heard, they are more likely to adhere to the agreed-upon principles. This democratic approach can begin with open discussions, brainstorming sessions, and workshops aimed at uncovering the core values of the group.

The content of ethical guidelines should address several key areas of group interactions. First and foremost, they should emphasize respect and dignity for all members. This includes recognizing individual contributions, protecting against discrimination, and promoting an environment where diverse perspectives are valued. Additionally, transparency in decision-making processes is paramount. Ethical guidelines should clearly outline how decisions are made, who is responsible, and how accountability will be maintained.

When contemplating ethical guidelines, it's crucial to consider the implications of power dynamics within the group. Power imbalances can lead to ethical lapses if not carefully managed. Guidelines should be explicit about the mechanisms to address and rectify unjust power hierarchies. This could involve setting up processes for conflict resolution, implementing anonymous reporting systems for breaches in ethics, or even revisiting leadership roles to ensure fairness and equity.

Moreover, confidentiality and data protection are becoming increasingly important in ethical considerations, especially in the era of digital communication and remote work. Guidelines should clearly state how sensitive information is to be handled, the safeguards in place to protect it, and the consequences of breaches. As technology continues to evolve, these guidelines may need revisiting to keep pace with new challenges and opportunities.

Ethical guidelines should also encompass the environmental and social responsibilities of the group. Whether it's a commitment to sustainable practices or a dedication to community engagement, these aspects reflect the broader impact of the group's activities. By integrating social responsibility into ethical frameworks, groups can align their operations with societal values and contribute positively to the world around them.

As teams transition from developing to implementing ethical guidelines, the role of leadership is pivotal. Leaders set the tone for ethical behavior through their actions and decisions. Therefore, they must embody the principles laid out in the guidelines and provide a model for others to follow. Effective leaders cultivate an atmosphere where ethical behavior is rewarded, and ethical dilemmas are addressed with integrity and transparency. This leadership stands as both a beacon and a benchmark for the team.

It is important that ethical guidelines remain dynamic documents, subject to periodic review and adaptation. Groups are not static entities; they evolve over time, encountering new challenges and opportunities that require reevaluation. Establishing regular intervals for review or creating a subcommittee devoted to ethics can ensure that guidelines remain relevant and useful. This ongoing commitment to ethical evolution helps groups to uphold their standards in an ever-changing landscape.

Furthermore, training and education play a vital role in the successful implementation of ethical guidelines. Offering regular workshops on ethics can help keep the guidelines at the forefront of group consciousness. By developing scenarios and exercises that simulate real-life ethical challenges, groups can prepare members to respond effectively when genuine dilemmas arise. Such proactive engagement builds a culture where ethical considerations become second nature.

Ultimately, the development of ethical guidelines in group dynamics is about cultivating a culture of trust, respect, and shared values. It requires the continuous and collaborative effort of all group members. When ethical principles are integrated into the very fabric of group interactions, they foster not only high performance but also satisfaction, cohesion, and a sense of purpose. As groups navigate the complexities of behavior and decision-making, well-crafted ethical guidelines serve as a compass, steering them towards collective success and sustainable impact.

Chapter 19:
Measuring Group Effectiveness

In the intricate dance of group dynamics, measuring effectiveness emerges as a pivotal element that anchors the success and sustainability of any collective endeavor. At its core, measuring group effectiveness involves not only spotting tangible outcomes but also appreciating those less visible dynamics that drive unity and progress. Key metrics, such as the achievement of shared goals, cohesion, and innovation, provide a roadmap for assessment. Equally important are the continuous improvement strategies that invite groups to engage in nimble reflection and adaptation. By establishing a robust framework of measurement, leaders and team members can harness transformational insights, fostering an environment of trust, accountability, and shared purpose. This chapter delves into the diverse metrics and strategies that illuminate paths to enhanced productivity and collaboration, inspiring every member of a group to contribute to a legacy of excellence and resilience.

Metrics for Success

In the complex terrain of group dynamics, where both chaos and synergy can coexist, the ability to measure success becomes paramount. Employing metrics that accurately reflect the effectiveness of a team can transform intuition into precision. This empowers leaders and members alike to navigate challenges with clarity. It's not just about spotting what's working; it's about identifying what needs fine-tuning and how to achieve sustainable growth together.

Understanding what truly constitutes success in a group setting requires a nuanced approach. It's tempting to rely solely on quantitative data, easy-to-calculate numbers that might offer clear-cut answers. However, truly impactful group effectiveness metrics blend quantitative with qualitative insights, allowing for a more comprehensive view. It's essential to consider performance outcomes, process optimization, and interpersonal dynamics.

Performance Outcomes: At the base of any metric for success is the outcome a group is working towards. Are the objectives met within the designated timeframe? Do the results align with expected quality standards? These questions, though straightforward, only scratch the surface. To genuinely gauge success, teams need to measure outcomes against the larger organizational purpose and their own stated mission.

When assessing outcomes, it involves more than just meeting deadlines and staying within budgets. It encompasses evaluating the impact of those outcomes. For instance, a sales team might achieve their quota, but understanding whether those sales lead to repeat business offers a deeper insight into true success. Metrics such as customer satisfaction and long-term client retention provide valuable data points.

Process Optimization: While results matter, how a group achieves those results is equally significant. Process-related metrics focus on efficiency, resource allocation, and workflow optimization. Consider the balance between effective systems and adaptability to change. Teams that excel are often those that maintain robust processes yet remain agile in the face of unforeseen circumstances.

Evaluating internal processes might include analyzing time spent on various tasks, resource utilization efficiency, or even the effectiveness of meetings. For example, employing surveys to understand if members feel their time in meetings is productive can provide immediate feedback. These insights can guide the refinement of processes, allowing teams to eliminate bottlenecks and improve collaboration.

Interpersonal Dynamics: The heart of group effectiveness often lies in the subtleties of interpersonal relationships. Measuring personal dynamics requires an understanding of collaboration, trust, and communication within the group. These human elements catalyze innovative thinking, enhance team morale, and ultimately affect the performance output.

Effective interpersonal dynamics can be evaluated through social network analysis, which observes the flow of information and communication among members. Surveys and 360-degree feedback processes also offer a glimpse into how team members perceive their interactions and their leaders' roles. High-trust environments tend to report higher engagement, reduced turnover, and increased creative output.

Alignment and Adaptability: Another critical metric is how well the group aligns with its goals and how adaptable it is to change. Alignment refers to the congruence between team objectives and individual roles. Every member ought to know not only their task but also how it fits into the larger picture. Meanwhile, adaptability metrics evaluate how swiftly and effectively a team can pivot in response to external pressures or internal failures.

Surveys assessing members' understanding of team goals and individual contributions, alongside assessments of the team's agility in past projects, paint a picture of how effectively the team aligns and adapts. Encouraging regular reflections and adjusting strategies according to feedback fosters a culture of continuous improvement.

Innovation and Creativity: In today's fast-paced environment, innovation isn't just an asset; it's a necessity. Metrics should capture the team's ability to sustain creativity and innovate consistently. Key indicators might include the number of new ideas generated, the frequency and diversity of brainstorming sessions, and the conversion rate of ideas into actionable projects.

For sustainable innovation, psychological safety is paramount, encouraging members to voice ideas without fear of criticism. A team that regularly brings forth new ideas yet struggles to implement them might be hindered by process inefficiencies or may require better cross-departmental collaboration.

Survey Tools and Analysis: Gathering data through well-designed surveys helps in transforming subjective perceptions into objective insights. Whether it involves pulse surveys for quick feedback or extensive annual reviews, survey tools can uncover hidden issues and highlight areas of success. Analyzing this data regularly keeps teams aligned with their goals and aware of areas that require attention.

Designing surveys to be specific—asking targeted questions about particular projects or general queries about workplace culture—yields actionable insights. This approach not only involves quantitative scales but also open-ended questions that capture the nuance of personal experience and perspectives.

Balancing Subjective and Objective Metrics: A balanced framework for success captures both the quantitative data—like task completion rates—and qualitative feedback on team experience. While hard data provide concrete benchmarks, the softer, subjective insights encapsulate the human experience of working within the group. Striking the right balance ensures a holistic appraisal of group effectiveness.

Utilizing focus groups or interviews complements data findings, offering richer context to numbers. This combinatory approach helps unravel whether numerical success comes at the cost of burnout or lack of cohesion, providing an opportunity for leaders to address issues before they escalate.

Continuous Feedback Loops: Finally, feedback shouldn't culminate in a single end-of-year report. Establishing ongoing feedback loops ensures that metrics remain dynamic and adjust to the rhythm of the team's evolution. Whether through periodic one-on-ones, retrospective meetings, or regular performance reviews, continuous feedback keeps the pulse of the team alive and the pathways open for ongoing development.

Integrating continuous feedback into the team culture fosters an environment where successes and setbacks become driving forces for learning. It promotes a growth mindset, encouraging members to see challenges as opportunities for improvement while celebrating achievements as milestones of their collective journey.

Through these diverse metrics, assessing group effectiveness becomes a multifaceted endeavor. It's not just about metrics in the abstract; it capacitates actionable insights driving genuine progress. Harnessing the power of appropriate metrics equips both leaders and teams with the knowledge they need to evolve, innovate, and ultimately achieve unprecedented success together.

Continuous Improvement Strategies

Continuous improvement is the heartbeat of any successful group, driving the ongoing evaluation and enhancement of group processes. It's not just about making changes for the sake of change; it requires a strategic approach, a commitment to reflection, and the courage to adapt. By fostering a culture where every member feels empowered to contribute ideas for betterment, groups can consistently evolve to meet challenges with agility and foresight.

One fundamental strategy for continuous improvement in measuring group effectiveness is the regular use of feedback loops. These loops function as cycles of assessment, feedback, and action. Encouraging open and honest dialogue allows group members to voice concerns, highlight successes, and suggest areas for improvement. This environment should be devoid of judgment, focusing instead on constructive criticism and collaborative problem-solving. Regularly scheduled feedback sessions enable this iterative process to become an embedded routine, benefitting the group as a whole.

Setting clear, measurable goals is another critical component. Goals act as benchmarks against which progress can be measured and realigned. These should be ambitious yet attainable, providing a roadmap that keeps all members focused on the collective vision. It's important to revisit these goals periodically, ensuring that they remain relevant in a continuously changing environment. When the group achieves a milestone, it's essential to celebrate successes to boost morale and reaffirm commitment to the journey ahead.

Engaging in after-action reviews can also significantly improve group effectiveness. After-action reviews are structured opportunities for team members to reflect on recent projects or activities. By discussing what worked, what didn't, and why, groups can gather insights that inform future endeavors. These reviews should be thorough yet concise, targeting both process and outcome, without getting bogged down in undue minutiae.

Another important strategy is the mindful integration of new tools and technologies. Leveraging technology doesn't mean adopting every new gadget or software; it entails making thoughtful choices about what's truly beneficial for the group. Digital tools can facilitate communication, streamline processes, and provide analytics that support decision-making. However, it's crucial to balance the human element with technological advancements to maintain a cohesive, motivated, and engaged team.

Flexibility is key to ongoing improvement. This means being willing to pivot strategies in response to new information or unforeseen challenges without being too rigid. Cultures that celebrate flexibility encourage innovative thinking, reducing resistance to change. Such adaptability can become a competitive advantage, ensuring the group isn't left behind in rapidly shifting landscapes.

Training and development should be considered as strategic investments in continuous improvement. Providing opportunities for team members to upskill can yield considerable dividends in terms of productivity and innovation. Whether through formal training sessions, workshops, or informal knowledge-sharing, fostering a culture of learning elevates the entire team's capabilities.

Regularly revisiting group dynamics and roles can also enhance effectiveness. The roles defined when a team is initially formed might need adjustments as projects evolve and members grow in their capabilities. Sometimes, simply shifting responsibilities or redefining roles can bring new life to a project, optimizing each member's contribution.

Establishing a system for recognizing and rewarding progress is crucial for sustaining improvement efforts. Acknowledgement of efforts, whether through formal recognition programs or informal praise, reinforces desired behaviors and motivates individuals to maintain high performance standards.

Finally, cultivating resilience within the group can serve as a bulwark against burnout and discouragement. Encouraging resilience involves promoting a healthy work-life balance, offering support systems like mentorship programs, and emphasizing the importance of both mental and physical wellbeing. Resilient teams are more likely to embrace change rather than resist it, turning challenges into opportunities for growth.

In summary, continuous improvement strategies encompass a broad array of practices, each crucial for the sustained effectiveness of any group. By embedding these practices into the fabric of group operations, they become more than just strategies; they become a way of life. This proactive approach ensures that groups remain dynamic, innovative, and primed to achieve their collective goals now and in the future.

Chapter 20:
The Role of Culture in Group Behavior

Culture acts as an invisible hand shaping how groups function, weaving its influences into every interaction and decision. It's like a backdrop that determines the norms and values the group embraces, impacting communication styles, conflict resolution, and even decision-making processes. In diverse environments, differing cultural perspectives can spark creativity, yet they can also challenge cohesion if not managed sensitively. Successful groups learn to navigate these differences, understanding that it's not just about merging distinct cultural traits, but about creating a new, inclusive culture—one that values diverse viewpoints while fostering unity. By embracing these dynamics, leaders can cultivate environments where cultural diversity serves as a strength rather than a barrier, unlocking the full potential of their teams. It's this intricate dance of cultural understanding that inspires collaboration and innovation, driving groups to achieve more together than they ever could alone.

Cultural Influences on Groups

In the tapestry of group dynamics, culture weaves itself as both backdrop and influence, shaping how groups form, interact, resolve conflicts, and strive towards achieving their goals. Culture can be defined as the shared patterns of behaviors, interactions, cognitive constructs, and understanding that are learned by socialization. This definition underscores the importance culture plays in the behavior of groups, whether familial, professional, or social. It's essential to understand that culture is not monolithic but multifaceted, varying significantly across different regions, ethnicities, and organizations.

When examining cultural influences on groups, it's helpful to consider both visible and invisible components of culture. Visible elements include language, dress, foods, and gestures—those facets of culture that are easily observed. On the other hand, invisible elements, such as beliefs, values, and thought patterns, hold a profound impact on group interactions and are usually more challenging to discern. For instance, how direct communication should be, comfort with hierarchy, and attitudes towards time can all significantly affect how a group functions.

Power distance, a critical cultural dimension identified by researcher Geert Hofstede, plays a substantial role in shaping group interactions. In cultures with high power distance, such as many in Asia and Latin America, hierarchy dictates how group members communicate and interact. Group members in such cultures might place great emphasis on respecting authority and maintaining harmony, often leading to top-down decision-making processes. Conversely, in low power distance cultures, such as the United States and Scandinavia, flatter organizational structures encourage open dialogue and criticism regardless of rank. This can foster innovation and creativity but might also lead to confusion or conflict when roles are not clearly defined.

Individualism versus collectivism is another cultural dimension that significantly influences group behavior. In individualistic cultures, group dynamics may prioritize personal goals over group objectives. These groups might reward individual achievements and encourage competition, fostering environments where members can thrive on personal innovation. On the contrary, collectivist cultures emphasize group harmony, cooperation, and consensus. Here, the group's success is synonymous with individual success, leading to more collaborative approaches to decision-making and problem-solving. Understanding these dynamics is vital for anyone looking to effectively lead or participate in multi-cultural teams.

Communication styles also drastically vary across cultures, impacting how teams understand and execute tasks. High-context cultures, such as Japan and many Arab countries, rely heavily on non-verbal cues and the broader context to convey meaning. Group members in these cultures may be adept at reading between the lines and interpreting subtleties, often communicating in indirect ways. In contrast, low-context cultures like Germany and the United States prioritize explicit communication. Here, clarity and precision are valued, with group dynamics favoring straightforward and unambiguous discussions.

Conflicts are inevitable in any group setting, yet culture can influence how conflict is perceived and managed. In some cultures, conflict is seen as a natural part of group life and an opportunity for growth and innovation. There, open debate and the expression of differing viewpoints are encouraged. In other cultures, particularly those in East Asia, maintaining harmony is paramount, and open conflict is often avoided. In these settings, conflict might be managed through indirect communication, mediation, or by subsuming individual desires for the sake of group cohesion.

Time orientation is another cultural factor that influences group behavior, affecting both the day-to-day functioning and long-term planning within groups. Cultures with a short-term orientation might prioritize immediate results and quick wins, focusing on short-term objectives and valuing flexibility and adaptability. Long-term oriented cultures, conversely, place importance on sustainability and persevering towards long-term results, valuing behaviors that promote thrift and perseverance.

The cultural background of a group can also significantly affect leadership styles and the acceptance of leadership within the group. Transformational leadership, which involves inspiring change and innovation through vision and charisma, might thrive in cultures that value individual achievements and new ideas. In contrast, transactional leadership, focusing on structured tasks, rewards, and processes, might be more effective in societies that value traditional hierarchies and established norms.

Modern globalization means that today's groups are often culturally diverse, bringing together people from various ethnicities, religions, and cultural backgrounds. This diversity holds potential for enriched perspectives and enhanced solutions, yet it also presents challenges that need carefully engineered strategies to manage. Building cultural competence in group settings involves understanding, respecting, and valuing the varied cultural backgrounds of all group members. By cultivating a space where all voices are heard, cultural diversity can be turned into a strength, enhancing the group's overall performance and cohesion.

Cultural influences are not only bound to ethnic or national backgrounds but also encompass organizational cultures. Organizations, much like nations, have their own sets of values and norms that influence group behavior. For instance, a corporate culture that encourages risk-taking and openness may promote a different group dynamic compared to one that prioritizes caution and stability. Leaders must be adept at navigating organizational cultures to harness and balance the diverse values that group members bring to the table.

Leaders managing culturally diverse teams benefit significantly from cultural intelligence, which combines knowledge of different cultural norms with the ability to appropriately and effectively adapt behaviors in response. Skilled leaders recognize the importance of cultural influences and are proactive in cultivating an inclusive atmosphere. They ensure that cultural differences are not only acknowledged but celebrated, creating teams where everyone feels valued and motivated.

In summary, cultural influences are deeply embedded in the fabric of group dynamics, molding everything from communication styles to conflict management and leadership. Successful group interactions in our increasingly interconnected world depend on recognizing and embracing these cultural influences. When culture is harnessed effectively, it can lead to more cohesive, innovative, and robust groups. Developing cultural competence within group settings is not simply a beneficial practice—it's a necessary one, propelling groups towards greater understanding and success in both local and global arenas.

Navigating Cultural Differences

Cultural differences in group behavior can be a double-edged sword. On one hand, they offer a rich tapestry of perspectives that can lead to innovation and creativity. On the other hand, they can create misunderstandings and conflict if not managed properly. Navigating these differences with sensitivity and awareness is crucial for the success of any team.

At the heart of cultural differences lies communication. Language barriers, diverse communication styles, and non-verbal cues can dramatically affect group dynamics. Imagine a situation where direct communication is valued in one culture while another prefers a more indirect approach. This disparity can lead to misinterpretations or, worse, offense. Moreover, nuances in body language, such as eye contact and gestures, may mean different things across cultures.

To bridge these cultural communication gaps, teams can benefit from adopting a mindset of curiosity and openness. Encouraging members to share their preferred communication styles helps in developing a shared understanding. This, in turn, can lead to more inclusive interactions and reduce the potential for friction. A simple strategy involves creating norms around communication, such as establishing guidelines for providing feedback or confirming understanding.

The concept of time also varies significantly across cultures and can impact group interactions. In some cultures, punctuality is a symbol of respect and professionalism. Conversely, other cultures may view time as more fluid and flexible. These differing views can lead to tensions in a group setting, particularly around meeting schedules and deadlines. Team leaders can navigate these differences by respecting cultural preferences while ensuring the team meets its objectives.

Decision-making processes are another area where cultural differences manifest. For instance, some cultures value collective consensus and emphasize group harmony, whereas others may prefer a more top-down, authoritative approach. These differences can influence how decisions are made and whose voices are heard. Leaders can address this by being explicit about decision-making processes and ensuring that each member feels valued and understood.

Power distance, or the extent to which less powerful members of a group accept and expect power disparity, is another cultural dimension worth noting. In high power-distance cultures, hierarchical structures are respected, and authority is rarely questioned. However, in low power-distance cultures, flat structures are favored, and feedback is encouraged. Understanding where a team member comes from on this spectrum helps in assigning roles and responsibilities that feel fair and appropriate to everyone.

Moreover, cultural differences can also dictate the level of assertiveness or modesty valued in a team setting. For some individuals, being outspoken is a sign of engagement and dedication; for others, it may be seen as disruptive. Leaders can benefit from recognizing and validating different modes of expression, balancing the need for vocal participation with the importance of listening and reflection.

Building cultural competence within a team isn't just a one-time initiative but an ongoing commitment. It requires continuous learning and adaptation. Workshops, cultural exchange programs, and reflective sessions can be instrumental in raising awareness and deepening understanding among team members. These initiatives can also foster an environment where cultural differences are not just tolerated but celebrated as a source of strength and resilience.

Additionally, aligning the team's goals with a shared vision that transcends cultural differences can unify diverse groups. When team members are focused on a collective objective, cultural distinctions become less about division and more about contributing to a greater collective wisdom. Cultivating a common purpose can help highlight the richness that diverse perspectives bring to problem-solving and innovation.

Recognizing and effectively managing cultural differences is not only about preventing conflicts but also about enhancing team performance. A culturally aware team can harness these differences to drive collaboration and innovation. Leaders and team members alike must commit to understanding and valuing the cultural backgrounds of each team member. This involves a willingness to both share one's own culture and understand others'. By doing so, the team can leverage the full spectrum of skills and experiences available, unlocking new potentials.

In today's globalized world, organizations often bring together individuals from a wide array of cultural backgrounds. As businesses expand, understanding how cultural differences affect group behavior will become even more critical. Those who succeed in this area will likely find themselves leading highly effective, innovative, and harmonious teams. In the journey to navigate cultural differences, it's crucial to remember that the process is as valuable as the outcome. By striving for cultural competence, teams can transform potential challenges into opportunities for growth.

Chapter 21:
Enhancing Team Development

Enhancing team development is a pivotal process that can transform a group of individuals into a cohesive and high-performing unit. It begins with understanding the natural stages of team development, from forming to performing, and recognizing that each stage presents unique challenges and opportunities for growth. Leaders play a crucial role in facilitating this progression by providing clear visions and aligning team goals with individual aspirations, fostering an environment where trust and open communication can flourish. By employing tools and strategies tailored to the team's specific needs—such as regular feedback loops, skill development workshops, and collaborative problem-solving sessions—leaders can cultivate resilience, adaptability, and collective competence. As members navigate through these stages, they learn to leverage their diverse strengths, thus driving innovation and achieving shared objectives. Ultimately, investing in team development doesn't just boost performance; it engenders a sense of belonging and mutual support, propelling the team towards sustained success and fulfillment.

Stages of Team Development

In the journey of enhancing team development, understanding the stages of team development is crucial. These stages serve as the building blocks for transforming a collection of individuals into a cohesive unit.

Recognizing these stages helps leaders and team members navigate the complexities of group dynamics, ultimately fostering a more effective team environment.

Bruce Tuckman's model of team development offers a well-regarded framework, outlining the stages as forming, storming, norming, performing, and adjourning. Each stage represents a distinct phase in team evolution, characterized by its own set of challenges and opportunities. By understanding these stages, teams can better anticipate obstacles and implement strategies to move forward efficiently.

In the *forming* stage, teams come together. It's a period marked by excitement and uncertainty as team members get acquainted with each other and the task at hand. During this phase, clarity in goals and roles is vital to set the foundation for future development. Leaders play an essential role here by facilitating introductions, articulating objectives, and establishing ground rules.

The subsequent stage, *storming*, often brings friction. Conflicts and clashes can arise as individuals express differing opinions and vie for positions within the group. These challenges are natural and crucial for progress. It's during this storming phase that team members begin to confront one another's ideas and assumptions, leading to a deeper understanding of the task and team dynamics. Effective conflict resolution and open communication strategies are paramount to navigating this stage successfully.

As teams overcome the turbulence of the storming phase, they move into the *norming* stage. Here, cohesion begins to develop. Roles become more clearly defined and accepted, and the team sets informal norms regarding how members will interact and work together. Trust starts to build, and collaboration improves, setting the stage for high performance.

When teams reach the *performing* stage, they operate at their peak capacity. With established norms and roles, team members collaborate seamlessly toward common objectives. Problem-solving becomes more effective, creativity flourishes, and productivity soars. Teams in this stage function with minimal supervision, as members are motivated and confident in achieving goals.

The final stage, *adjourning*, also known as the mourning stage, marks the completion of the project or the team's disbandment. It's a phase that can bring mixed emotions. Pride in achievements and sadness over the team's dissolution often coexist. This stage emphasizes the importance of celebrating accomplishments and providing closure. Leaders should facilitate reflection on lessons learned and recognize individual contributions to foster a sense of accomplishment and prepare team members for future collaborations.

Understanding and navigating these stages can significantly enhance a team's development and effectiveness. Each phase presents opportunities to learn and grow, both individually and collectively. By skillfully managing the dynamics at play in each stage, leaders and team members can create a resilient team capable of overcoming challenges and achieving exceptional outcomes.

Also, it's worth noting that these stages aren't always linear. Teams may find themselves revisiting earlier stages due to changes in team composition, new projects, or significant external influences. Flexibility and adaptability are crucial qualities for team leadership to address such instances effectively. By being aware of the dynamics at each stage, teams can pivot and realign to continue progressing towards their goals.

Finally, tools like team-building exercises, reflective practices, and feedback loops can assist in progressing through these stages. By fostering an environment where open communication and trust are prioritized, teams can more readily navigate the complexities of development. These practices not only enhance team performance but also contribute to each member's personal growth and satisfaction.

In conclusion, learning about the stages of team development provides valuable insights into the intricate dance of team dynamics. This knowledge equips teams with a roadmap to guide their evolution, ultimately transforming initial potential into solidified performance. When teams are attuned to these stages, they unlock their full capacity to operate effectively in the ever-changing landscape of modern collaboration.

Tools for Fostering Team Growth

As teams evolve through various stages of development, the tools and strategies employed to foster growth and cohesion become paramount. These tools act as catalysts, driving collaboration, innovation, and resilience. Understanding and utilizing these tools effectively can aid in steering a team towards its full potential. The significance of such mechanisms lies not just in their application but also in the timing and manner of their deployment. When applied judiciously, these tools can transform challenges into opportunities for growth.

One of the primary tools for fostering team growth is effective communication. While this might sound straightforward, the depth of its impact cannot be overstated. Clear communication channels ensure that every team member understands their role and responsibilities while being attuned to the collective objectives of the group. Establishing regular check-ins or stand-ups can enhance transparency and help preempt misunderstandings and conflicts. This practice encourages an open forum for feedback, allowing team members to voice concerns or ideas without fear of judgment.

Moreover, leveraging technology to augment communication can significantly enhance connectivity, especially for dispersed teams. Tools like video conferencing platforms, collaborative document editors, and project management software can keep everyone on the same page irrespective of physical location. The integration of such technology not only facilitates seamless collaboration but also empowers team members by providing them with the tools they need to succeed.

Emphasizing personal and professional development is another critical aspect. When team members feel that their growth is prioritized, it translates into higher engagement levels. Providing opportunities for training, workshops, and seminars can bridge skill gaps and keep the team agile in the face of evolving challenges. Moreover, encouraging cross-training within teams can foster empathy and understanding, as team members gain insight into each other's roles and challenges.

An often-underestimated tool for team growth is the cultivation of a positive team culture. This involves creating an environment where mutual respect, support, and a shared sense of purpose thrive. Leaders play an instrumental role here by exemplifying the values and behaviors they wish to see. Celebrating successes, however small, and learning from failures without assigning blame can nurture a resilient mindset that embraces growth.

Constructive feedback mechanisms should be embedded within the team's fabric. Feedback should be seen not as criticism but as a vital tool for growth. By fostering an environment of psychological safety, team members are encouraged to learn from their mistakes and build on their successes. Regular one-on-one sessions between team leaders and members can serve as a platform for feedback exchange, setting personal goals, and aligning individual objectives with team priorities.

Diversifying the team's skill set is another potent strategy. Diversity extends beyond demographic factors to include diverse thought processes, experiences, and skills. A team enriched with various perspectives is better equipped to approach problems creatively and innovatively. Encouraging the hiring and inclusion of members from various backgrounds can lead to richer discussions and more comprehensive solutions.

Motivation, both intrinsic and extrinsic, acts as a compelling driver of team performance and growth. While intrinsic motivation is fueled by personal satisfaction and alignment with personal values and goals, extrinsic motivation often comes from recognition, rewards, and incentives. Tailoring motivational strategies to meet individual team member's aspirations can amplify their commitment to the team's goals.

Regularly revisiting and realigning team goals can keep the team focused and motivated. In a dynamic environment, goals might need to be adapted or redefined to stay relevant. These sessions not only reaffirm the team's direction but also provide an opportunity to acknowledge and reset priorities collaboratively.

The leadership's role in fostering team growth cannot be overemphasized. Effective leaders act as facilitators, guiding the team through challenges while enabling each member to shine. Leadership development is a continuous process, and investing in leadership training can bolster the capacity to lead with empathy, vision, and adaptability.

Lastly, measuring the impact of these tools and strategies helps in understanding what works and what does not. Metrics that gauge team cohesion, morale, productivity, and individual growth provide insights into the health of the team. These metrics serve as a feedback loop, enabling leaders to make data-informed decisions to spur further growth.

In conclusion, fostering team growth is an intricate tapestry woven with diverse threads of communication, culture, motivation, and leadership. By strategically employing these tools, teams not only enhance their immediate performance but also build a foundation for sustained success. The journey of team development is one of continuous learning and adaptation, where the collective strength of the team is harnessed to navigate the complexities of modern challenges.

Chapter 22:
The Future of Team Collaboration

As we gaze into the horizon of team collaboration, it becomes vital for leaders and innovators to embrace a future where agility and adaptability serve as the keystones. The landscape is shaped by a convergence of advanced technologies and evolving social paradigms, propelling teams into realms once thought improbable. The integration of artificial intelligence, automation, and virtual reality is reshaping interactions, requiring a profound shift in how trust and collaboration are cultivated. Emerging trends hint at increasingly fluid team structures, blending diverse skills to solve complex problems with unmatched creativity and efficiency. Future-ready teams will thrive on inclusivity and a willingness to break traditional hierarchies, crafting a culture where every voice holds transformative potential. Preparing for these challenges involves nurturing emotional intelligence, fostering an environment of psychological safety, and leveraging digital platforms for seamless communication. The journey ahead calls for visionary leadership and a collaborative spirit that transcends geographic and cultural boundaries.

Trends in Group Dynamics

As we venture into an era where the landscape of team collaboration is continually evolving, understanding the trends in group dynamics becomes crucial. The shifting nature of work environments, coupled with rapid technological advancements, has profoundly influenced how groups form, interact, and thrive. Today's groups are more dynamic, fluid, and complex than ever, and keeping abreast of these changes is key for anyone involved in collective work.

One significant trend shaping group dynamics is the increasing prevalence of diverse, multicultural teams. As globalization accelerates, the necessity for teams to comprise individuals from varied backgrounds is more prominent. Diversity brings a wealth of perspectives and ideas, enhancing creativity and problem-solving abilities. However, it also poses challenges, such as overcoming cultural misunderstandings and biases. The ability to harness diversity positively impacts group performance, but it requires intentional strategies in fostering an inclusive atmosphere where every voice is heard and valued.

Another trend is the shift towards more decentralized and autonomous teams. Traditional hierarchical structures are being replaced by flatter organizations, where decision-making is distributed across team members rather than being concentrated in a single leader. This decentralization fosters a sense of ownership and empowerment among team members, encouraging innovation and agility. However, it also requires a robust framework for accountability and clear channels of communication to ensure alignment with the broader organizational goals.

The role of emotional intelligence (EI) in group dynamics is also gaining recognition as a critical driver of team success. Emotional intelligence involves the ability to understand one's own emotions and those of others, facilitating effective interpersonal interactions. Teams with high EI tend to demonstrate greater empathy, conflict resolution skills, and collaboration, ultimately leading to improved team cohesion and performance. As such, organizations are increasingly prioritizing EI development in their training programs.

Technological innovations are markedly reshaping how groups collaborate. The rise of digital tools, such as collaborative platforms and project management software, has transformed teamwork into a more streamlined and efficient process. Tools like Slack, Trello, and Zoom have become indispensable for enabling communication and coordination across distances. However, dependence on technology also introduces challenges, such as cybersecurity risks and the potential for digital burnout. Balancing the benefits and drawbacks of technology is an ongoing challenge that teams must navigate.

Virtual and remote collaboration has surged, accelerated by the global shift towards remote work. The ability to work from anywhere opens up opportunities to tap into a global talent pool, but it also requires new competencies in managing virtual teams. Teams need to establish strong virtual collaboration systems, emphasize clear communication, and foster trust to overcome the lack of physical presence. Flexibility in managing different time zones and cultural variations also plays a crucial role in the effectiveness of remote teams.

There is also a growing focus on sustainability and ethical practices within group dynamics. Groups are increasingly recognizing their role in contributing positively to society and the environment, pushing for sustainable practices and ethical decision-making. This trend reflects not only societal expectations but also the values of younger generations entering the workforce. Ensuring that group goals align with ethical standards and sustainability objectives is becoming integral to long-term success.

Empathy and well-being at work are receiving unprecedented attention as organizations realize the impact of mental health on group productivity. Companies are adopting initiatives to support mental health and ensure a healthy work-life balance, recognizing that well-cared-for employees are more engaged and productive. Strategies like flexible working hours, mental health days, and stress management programs are being implemented to prioritize the holistic well-being of groups.

The trend towards cross-functional collaboration is another dynamic transforming group interactions. Interdisciplinary teams are formed to tackle complex projects, bringing together individuals with varied skills and expertise. This diversity in functionality enhances creativity but demands cohesive collaboration and communication across different areas of knowledge. The ability to integrate diverse skills effectively determines the success of these collaborative efforts.

Lastly, agility in group dynamics is increasingly valued. In an ever-changing landscape, teams are required to be adaptable, continuously learning and evolving to meet new challenges. Agile methodologies, originally developed for software development, are now being applied broadly to improve project management and team productivity. These approaches emphasize iterative progress, flexibility, and collaboration, equipping teams with the resilience needed to thrive amidst uncertainty.

To prepare for the future of team collaboration, individuals and organizations must remain open to embracing these trends. Building resilient teams that can adapt to rapid changes while maintaining cohesiveness and motivation is critical. Leaders play a pivotal role in guiding their teams through these transformations, fostering environments where innovation and collaboration can flourish. By understanding and anticipating these trends, teams can strategically position themselves to harness the full potential of collective efforts for future success.

Preparing for Future Challenges

As we look ahead, preparing teams for future challenges isn't just a necessity—it's a strategic advantage. The landscape of collaboration is rapidly evolving, shaped by continuous technological advancements, shifting workplace dynamics, and global trends. Teams that are adaptable and prepared are more likely to thrive in the face of uncertainty and change. The key lies in understanding and leveraging the drivers of change, fostering a culture of resilience, and equipping teams with the tools they need to navigate complexities.

One of the first steps in preparing for future challenges is recognizing the pivotal role technology will play. Technological innovation is both a driving force and a disruptor in how teams operate. Digital tools designed for collaboration, such as real-time communication platforms and project management software, have already transformed how we work together. However, the pace of technological change means teams must remain open to continuous learning. Embracing new technologies can lead to enhanced productivity, but it requires a commitment to ongoing training and development.

Moreover, as artificial intelligence and machine learning become more integrated into workplace tools, team members will need to develop a nuanced understanding of how to collaborate with these technologies. Rather than viewing AI as a competitor, teams should see it as a partner that can augment their capabilities. This shift in perspective necessitates a proactive approach to skill development, ensuring that team members are equipped to leverage AI effectively. Additionally, ethical considerations around technology use must be at the forefront of strategic planning.

Flexibility and adaptability are also paramount in the face of future challenges. The ability to pivot in response to unexpected changes will define successful teams. This doesn't just mean having flexible policies in place, but also fostering a mindset of agility within the team. Encouraging experimentation and allowing for failure as part of the learning process can cultivate a culture where adaptability thrives.

Leaders play a crucial role in setting this tone, guiding their teams with both vision and adaptability.

Alongside technological and strategic preparedness, emotional resilience can't be overlooked. The psychological readiness of team members is as important as their technical skills. Teams that prioritize emotional well-being and create supportive environments are better positioned to handle stress and uncertainty. This involves promoting open communication, offering support resources, and recognizing the importance of mental health. Emotional intelligence training can empower team members to be more aware of their own emotions and those of others, which is crucial during times of change.

Another vital aspect of preparing for future challenges is fostering inclusivity and diversity. Diverse teams bring a variety of perspectives and solutions, which can be highly advantageous in problem-solving and innovation. It's essential to create an environment where all voices are heard and contributed to decision-making processes. This not only enriches the team's capabilities but also builds resilience, as diverse teams are often better able to adapt to and manage change.

In addition, as the structure of teams becomes more fluid, with hybrid and remote models becoming the norm, leaders must focus on maintaining cohesive team dynamics. This includes rethinking leadership styles to be inclusive of remote management strategies and ensuring that team bonds remain strong despite physical distances. It requires investing in tools and practices that bridge gaps, whether through virtual team-building activities or refined digital communication platforms. Ensuring that every team member feels connected and valued, regardless of their location, is essential for future preparedness.

Finally, strategic foresight and scenario planning are invaluable in anticipating future challenges. While we can't predict every change, teams can build a framework for anticipating potential scenarios and outcomes. This involves identifying key trends, both within and outside the organization, and assessing their implications. Teams should engage in regular strategic reviews, using foresight to inform their plans and decisions. By visualizing different future scenarios, teams can develop strategic responses that are both proactive and reactive.

In conclusion, preparing for future challenges requires a holistic approach encompassing technological fluency, emotional resilience, adaptability, inclusivity, and strategic foresight. Teams that proactively invest in these areas are not just equipped to survive; they are poised to innovate and excel. In a world marked by unpredictability, the strength of a team lies in its readiness to embrace the future, whatever it may hold.

Chapter 23:
Case Studies in Group Success

In the ever-evolving landscape of team dynamics, the chronicles of successful groups provide rich insights into the mechanics of collaboration. Take, for instance, the story of a small tech startup that blossomed into an industry leader by leveraging a culture of open communication and shared vision. Their success wasn't just about having innovative ideas; it hinged on a robust framework of trust and inclusivity, encouraging team members to voice diverse perspectives. In contrast, a healthcare team facing a daunting crisis illustrated the power of adaptive leadership and resilience in the face of adversity. By prioritizing flexibility and empathetic communication, they navigated complex challenges and emerged stronger. These case studies reveal that while methods may vary, foundational elements like mutual respect, adaptability, and shared goals are pivotal in transforming ordinary groups into extraordinary success stories. The lessons learned underscore that fostering an environment where each member feels valued can be the catalyst for exceptional group achievements. Together, these narratives showcase what is possible when collective potential is harnessed effectively.

Analysis of Successful Teams

Successful teams often function through a seamless interplay of various elements that align towards a single set of goals. But what is it that sets them apart? How do a handful of groups emerge not just competent, but extraordinary? At the core of these successful formations are several critical features that, when woven together, create resilient and high-performing teams.

One key characteristic of successful teams is their unwavering clarity of purpose and shared vision. This sense of purpose aligns each team member's efforts, reinforcing individual commitment to the collective objectives. Consider a sports team that continuously strategizes and rehearses, not just for the victory of a single game, but as part of a larger pursuit of excellence or championship glory. The athletes have a clear, mutual understanding of their roles and objectives, which ignites their drive and dedication. It's evident that when a team possesses a strong shared vision, their collective potential is magnified.

Besides a shared vision, successful teams master the art of effective communication. Open channels of communication ensure that ideas flow freely and challenges are tackled before they become insurmountable obstacles. Regular feedback mechanisms, whether through structured meetings or open dialogue, cultivate an environment where every voice is heard and valued. In high-stakes environments like emergency response teams, seamless communication can mean the difference between life and death. They utilize structured protocols to ensure that the right information reaches the right individuals at the right time, showcasing how crucial communication is for success.

The allocation and embracing of individual strengths bring another profound dimension to team success. In successful teams, members are encouraged to leverage their unique skills and talents while being mindful of others' expertise. This collective strength leads to a more dynamic and capable group. Think about tech companies renowned for innovation; they bring together diverse experts who each excel in their specialized fields. By drawing on this reservoir of varied expertise, these teams tackle complex problems with innovative solutions.

Leadership, of course, plays an instrumental role. Effective leaders are not mere figures of authority; they inspire, mentor, and guide. They lead by example, demonstrating commitment and integrity. In projects where outcomes continue to surpass expectations, look closely, and you'll find leaders who empower their teams, fostering a sense of ownership and accountability among members. Whether a leader steps in to mediate conflicts or recognizes the team's achievements, their actions ripple through the group, catalyzing positive group dynamics.

Another pillar of successful teams is their resilience in the face of adversity. Resilient teams have cultivated an adaptive mindset that allows them to navigate unexpected challenges with poise and without derailing from their core mission. Establishing a supportive culture, where failure is viewed as a learning opportunity rather than a dead-end, strengthens the team's ability to bounce back stronger. This was evident in organizations that weathered financial crises, transforming setbacks into growth opportunities by re-evaluating strategies and implementing necessary changes.

The role of trust cannot be overstated when examining successful teams. Trust is the glue that binds team members, enabling them to collaborate more openly and effectively. It fosters a sense of safety that encourages taking risks and sharing bold ideas without fear of ridicule. Building such trust takes time and consistent effort, yet its presence unlocks new levels of collaboration and creativity. In environments like research teams, where cutting-edge ideas surface regularly, trust among members allows for synergy and collaborative breakthroughs.

Diversity within a team also contributes significantly to its success. Diverse teams bring a rich tapestry of perspectives, enhancing creativity and problem-solving capacities. When individuals from varied backgrounds and experiences unite, they challenge each other's assumptions and spur innovation. Take global corporations, known for devising products that cater to international markets, which actively cultivate diverse teams that reflect the diversity of their consumer base. This inclusivity not only drives innovation but also equips teams to be more culturally attuned and empathetic to the needs of diverse customers.

Another distinguishing factor is the team's approach to continuous learning. Successful teams are not satisfied with their current level of expertise; they commit to constant improvement. By fostering an environment conducive to learning, be it through workshops, training sessions, or reflective practices, team members are encouraged to expand their knowledge and skills. This dedication to growth ensures that teams remain competitive and forward-looking, adeptly adjusting to emerging trends and technologies.

Goals, when structured effectively, play a pivotal role in defining a team's success trajectory. Successful teams set SMART (Specific, Measurable, Achievable, Relevant, Time-bound) goals that not only clarify intentions but also map the path to achievement. The use of these clear benchmarks allows teams to track their progress, celebrate small victories, and recalibrate strategies when necessary. These goals become the milestones that guide the team, urging members onward in a collective journey of relentless pursuit.

Moreover, successful teams are agile, fostering environments where adaptation and flexibility are embraced. In today's fast-paced world, where disruption can occur with little warning, the capacity to pivot quickly is invaluable. Agile teams are not paralyzed by rapid changes; instead, they adjust their strategies to align with evolving conditions, maintaining momentum and sustaining progress.

In essence, successful teams are a symphony of diverse, aligned, and empowered individuals working under effective leadership towards common objectives. They are ever-evolving entities, continuously learning and adapting to maintain their edge amid a plethora of challenges. By examining these elements, one discerns that certain attributes are consistently present, yet the unique application of these attributes speaks to the distinctiveness of every successful team. The study of these attributes offers powerful insights and practical lessons for any individual or organization seeking to cultivate success within their own teams.

Lessons Learned from Effective Groups

Delving into the intricacies of successful groups, it's intriguing to see recurring patterns and key components that universally contribute to their effectiveness. When we look carefully at what makes certain groups excel, we gain valuable insights that can be applied across various contexts, from corporate boardrooms to grassroots community initiatives.

In studying group success stories, one of the most notable lessons revolves around the power of shared vision and purpose. Groups that achieve remarkable outcomes often start with a clear, compelling direction. This shared vision acts as a guiding star, aligning individual efforts towards a common goal. It fosters unity and helps teams navigate through challenges with a collective determination.

Moreover, effective groups tend to nurture an environment where open communication thrives. Within these groups, colleagues are not only encouraged but expected to voice their thoughts and opinions. This openness leads to richer discussions and innovative solutions. It also creates a culture of trust, where members feel safe to share ideas without fear of judgment or dismissal.

Another critical lesson is the balance between leadership and autonomy. Successful groups acknowledge the importance of strong leadership, yet they also empower members to make decisions within their areas of expertise. This balance promotes a dynamic where leaders set the course, but individuals feel a sense of ownership over their contributions. It's a delicate interplay that maximizes the strengths of each member while preserving cohesive direction.

In addition to leadership, the adaptability of effective groups cannot be overstated. These teams are resilient and demonstrate a remarkable ability to pivot when necessary. They embrace change rather than resist it, viewing new challenges as opportunities for growth. This adaptability is often cultivated through a culture that values continuous learning and development, both on an individual and collective level.

Diversity also emerges as a powerful driver of group success. Diverse teams bring together a mosaic of perspectives, skills, and experiences that can lead to more creative solutions. They challenge conventional thinking and push the boundaries of what's possible, leading to outcomes that homogenous groups might not achieve. However, it's important to note that diversity alone isn't sufficient; it must be coupled with inclusivity to harness its full potential.

Conflict, although often viewed negatively, is another area from which effective groups draw strength. These groups understand that conflict is natural and, when managed properly, can be constructive. They implement strategies to address disagreements openly and respectfully, transforming potential friction points into opportunities for deeper understanding and stronger collaboration.

Equally vital is the commitment to accountability within successful groups. Members hold themselves and each other accountable for contributing to the group's goals. There's a mutual understanding that each individual's performance impacts the collective result. This culture of accountability is underpinned by clearly defined roles and responsibilities, as well as measurable objectives and feedback loops.

Additionally, effective groups have a remarkable ability to maintain focus on long-term objectives while tackling immediate tasks. This dual focus ensures that while the everyday operations are attended to, they also remain aligned with overarching goals. It requires a disciplined approach to planning and prioritizing, allowing teams to adapt to short-term demands without losing sight of their long-term vision.

Another insightful lesson is the emphasis on well-being and morale. Successful groups tend to cultivate a supportive atmosphere where members feel valued and appreciated. High morale is often linked to higher productivity and increased creativity. These groups recognize the importance of celebrating achievements and providing emotional support during challenging times.

Finally, effective groups rely on continuous reflection and adaptation to sustain their success. They regularly evaluate their processes and outcomes, learning from both successes and failures. This continuous improvement mindset ensures that they remain agile and competitive in ever-changing environments.

In conclusion, the lessons gleaned from effective groups provide a roadmap for anyone seeking to enhance group dynamics and outcomes. By embracing a shared vision, fostering open communication, balancing leadership with autonomy, valuing diversity, managing conflict constructively, maintaining accountability, and continuously adapting, groups can navigate the complexities of collaboration with greater ease and achievement. Through these practices, the collective power of groups can be harnessed to achieve not only success but transformative impact.

Chapter 24:
Practical Applications
of Group Psychology

In the realm of group psychology, theory finds its profound significance in practical application, as it is here that abstract concepts transform into tangible outcomes. When we apply the principles of group dynamics to real-world situations, such as in corporate environments, community organizations, or educational settings, we unlock a powerful toolkit for enhancing interaction and collaboration. By understanding the subtle ebbs and flows of group behavior, leaders and team members can create more cohesive and effective teams. For instance, implementing structured decision-making processes not only boosts overall productivity but also ensures a diverse range of voices are heard and valued. These strategies enhance motivation and morale, paving the way for innovation and resilience in the face of challenges. With practical insights into fostering trust, managing conflict, and embracing diversity, practitioners of group psychology can transform potential discord into synergistic harmony, ultimately driving collective success in a world where interconnectedness reigns supreme.

Real-World Applications

In an ever-evolving world where collaboration is key, understanding group psychology offers valuable insights that can be applied across various contexts. Whether you're steering a business toward success, aiming to enhance educational outcomes, or leading community initiatives, the principles of group psychology can transform aspirations into reality. Real-world applications of these principles illuminate how individuals and organizations can harness collective behaviors to achieve remarkable outcomes.

In the corporate realm, the application of group psychology is paramount. Consider a business aiming to launch a new product. The team's ability to collaborate effectively, communicate openly, and integrate diverse insights can significantly influence the product's success. Leaders who understand group dynamics aspire to create an environment where members feel valued and heard. They employ team-building exercises to foster trust, lay ground rules for effective communication, and establish a shared vision. The outcome? Teams that not only meet but often exceed expectations, driving innovation and competitive advantage.

Education is another sphere where group psychology finds profound application. Classrooms aren't just spaces for individual learning; they're microcosms of society where students learn to navigate group dynamics. Teachers who apply group psychology principles create collaborative learning environments. They encourage group projects, discussions, and peer assessments, fostering critical thinking and communication skills. By embedding group psychology into teaching methods, educators prepare students not just academically but socially, equipping them for the collaborative demands of the real world.

In healthcare, group psychology enhances both patient and staff experiences. Multidisciplinary teams in hospitals embody the power of group dynamics. These teams, consisting of doctors, nurses, and specialists, pool their diverse expertise to develop comprehensive patient care plans. Understanding how to navigate potential conflicts and communicate effectively ensures that patient care is coordinated and efficient. Moreover, fostering a cohesive team environment reduces burnout and increases job satisfaction among healthcare workers, ultimately improving patient outcomes.

Non-profit organizations and community initiatives also benefit from these principles. Whether it's organizing a community clean-up or advocating for policy change, leaders who understand group dynamics can mobilize volunteers and stakeholders more effectively. Clear communication about goals and the impact of participation increases engagement, while strategies for conflict resolution maintain harmony and sustain group momentum. In this way, group psychology doesn't just facilitate participation; it transforms collective effort into tangible social change.

Sports teams provide a vivid demonstration of group psychology in action. Successful teams aren't just a collection of talented individuals; they're units that understand trust, communication, and motivation. Coaches who leverage group psychology principles work on building team cohesion and resilience. By creating an environment where each player's strengths are recognized and utilized, coaches enhance the team's overall performance. This understanding transforms players into a well-oiled machine, achieving greater heights together than they could individually.

In creative industries, such as advertising and film, group psychology fosters innovation. Creative projects thrive on the amalgamation of diverse ideas, perspectives, and talents. Leaders in these fields use psychological insights to cultivate an atmosphere where creativity can flourish—spaces where team members feel safe to express ideas without fear of judgment. Here, the psyches of individuals united under a common goal unleash a torrent of creative potential, leading to groundbreaking projects that captivate audiences.

Even in personal relationships, understanding group dynamics can make a significant difference. Families and friendships operate as mini-groups; recognizing the dynamics within them—such as roles, communication styles, and emotional influences—can strengthen bonds. By applying conflict resolution techniques and fostering open communication, individuals can navigate challenges more gracefully, ensuring healthier and more fulfilling relationships.

A notable sphere where group psychology's principles are vital is crisis management. Whether a natural disaster or an organizational emergency, the effectiveness of the response hinges on the ability of groups to work together under pressure. Crisis leaders who understand group psychology can maintain team cohesion and focus. They implement strategies that support resilience, allowing teams to navigate the complexity of the crisis more effectively and recover more quickly.

On a global scale, international collaborations in addressing climate change, technological advancements, or health crises benefit immensely from group psychology. Multinational teams confront the challenge of navigating cultural diversity to reach consensus. Leaders who grasp cultural nuances and group dynamics can mediate differences, not as barriers, but as opportunities for richer, more comprehensive solutions. By appreciating diverse perspectives and fostering inclusive dialogue, these teams can tackle intricacies of global issues with enhanced creativity and effectiveness.

Through these myriad applications, it's clear that group psychology is more than just an academic concept; it's a toolkit for transforming the dynamics of collaboration into formidable forces for change and progress. By integrating these insights into practice, individuals, teams, and organizations can navigate complex scenarios with finesse and achieve extraordinary outcomes in the interconnected web of modern society.

Implementing Group Strategies

In the realm of group psychology, effectively applying strategies designed to harness the collective power of a group is as much an art as it is a science. Group strategies are not a one-size-fits-all solution; they are dynamic and must be tailored to fit the unique composition and goals of each group. By focusing on the application of theoretical knowledge in practical settings, individuals and organizations can maximize their collective potential. This requires a thorough understanding of the group's objectives, the specific challenges they face, and the individual dynamics at play.

One key strategy for implementing effective group strategies is fostering an environment that promotes open communication and psychological safety. Members of a group are more likely to contribute openly and take creative risks when they feel safe and respected. This involves establishing norms that encourage respectful dialogue and active listening. Leaders can facilitate this environment by modeling appropriate behavior and addressing any misconduct promptly and effectively. When team members feel heard, they are more likely to engage wholeheartedly, enhancing the group's overall function.

Another critical component in implementing group strategies is ensuring clarity of purpose. Each member should have a clear understanding of the group's goals and how their individual roles support these objectives. This clarity not only aligns team efforts but also empowers members to take initiative, knowing how their contributions fit into the broader scheme. Creating shared goals can also help reduce friction because team members can rally around a common objective, transcending personal differences or preferences. Regular revisiting of these goals allows for recalibration as the team evolves or as project requirements change.

Leadership plays a pivotal role in the successful application of group strategies. Effective leaders not only direct the team towards achieving its goals but also nurture the potential within each team member. They recognize the diverse skills and perspectives each member brings and actively encourage their expression. Leadership is not just about giving directions; it's about inspiring trust, motivating team members, and communicating a vision that resonates with everyone involved. By maintaining focus on both task achievement and team welfare, leaders can steer the team through challenges and toward success.

To implement group strategies effectively, it is also essential to tap into the diverse strengths and perspectives of team members. This involves recognizing the value that each individual brings and leveraging these differences as a source of innovation and problem-solving. Diversity can drastically enhance decision-making processes and outcomes, drawing upon a broad range of experiences and viewpoints. Strategies, therefore, must be inclusive and engage all members by valuing their contributions, which can increase satisfaction and reduce turnover.

In addition to leveraging interpersonal dynamics and diversity, practical tools such as regular team meetings, defined roles, and timelines provide structure that aids in the implementation of group strategies. Regular check-ins allow teams to stay aligned and swiftly address any arising issues. Clearly defined roles reduce ambiguity and inter-role conflict, enabling members to focus on their tasks effectively. Moreover, timelines ensure that objectives are pursued with urgency and milestones help in maintaining momentum and providing a sense of achievement.

Establishing feedback mechanisms is another strategic measure to ensure that group strategies are effectively implemented. Constructive feedback loops enable continuous learning and improvement by keeping the group aware of what is working well and what might need adjustment. Feedback should be specific, timely, and oriented towards growth, rather than criticism. When feedback is incorporated regularly and thoughtfully, it empowers group members, fostering an adaptive and proactive team culture.

Another strategy involves leveraging technology to enhance collaboration and communication. Digital tools can support many aspects of group function, from project management to real-time communication across different locations. Technology can break down geographical barriers and facilitate the seamless exchange of ideas, allowing teams to operate cohesively even when physically dispersed. However, while technology can be a boon, it is essential to choose platforms that suit the team's particular needs and to ensure that all members are proficient in using them.

Conflict resolution skills are indispensable for implementing group strategies. Conflict is a natural part of any collaborative process but must be managed effectively to avoid derailing group efforts. Proactive conflict resolution involves recognizing differing perspectives, facilitating constructive dialogue, and finding mutually beneficial solutions. By addressing conflicts promptly and skillfully, a group can turn potential disruptions into opportunities for growth and innovation.

Group strategies should also incorporate motivation techniques tailored to the team's unique composition. Motivation can be driven by diverse factors including recognition, personal development, and reward systems. Understanding these motivational drivers allows strategies to be fine-tuned, ensuring high levels of engagement and productivity. Leaders can enhance motivation by setting challenging but attainable goals, recognizing achievements, and fostering a sense of belonging within the team.

Finally, for group strategies to be successful, they must be both adaptable and sustainable. Flexibility is key in adapting strategies to changing circumstances or pivoting when traditional tactics fail.

Sustainability refers to developing strategies that are not overly reliant on exhaustive resources or that lead to burnout. By fostering a balance between innovation and steadfast consistency, groups can remain resilient and effective over the long term.

Ultimately, the implementation of group strategies hinges on a commitment to understanding and harnessing the intricacies of human behavior within a collective context. This involves a continuous cycle of assessment, implementation, feedback, and adaptation. By thoughtfully combining these elements, individuals and organizations can unlock the full potential of group dynamics, leading to transformative results in both individual and collective realms.

Chapter 25:
Mastering the Power
of Group Interactions

In the world of group dynamics, mastering the art of interaction stands as a beacon for both personal and professional growth. When individuals come together, the potential for synergy is limitless, fostering an environment ripe for innovation and profound achievement. This intricate dance of communication, collaboration, and mutual influence requires an acute understanding of both the overt and subtle nuances that drive group behavior. By focusing one's efforts on refining interaction skills, embracing diverse perspectives, and nurturing the collective intelligence of the group, leaders and team members alike can unlock an array of long-term benefits. These include heightened productivity, enriched relationships, and a sustained sense of belonging and purpose. As you hone these strengths, remember that the mastery of group interactions is not a finite goal but a continuous journey that empowers you to adapt and thrive amid the complex tapestry of human connection.

Strategies for Personal and Professional Growth

Mastering the power of group interactions is more than an academic exercise or professional requirement; it's a pathway to profound personal and professional transformation. When individuals become adept at navigating group dynamics, they unlock a range of opportunities for growth that extend well beyond the immediate context of teamwork. By understanding how groups function and employing strategic approaches to interactions, one can foster an environment where personal development and professional advancement are natural outcomes.

First off, demonstrating effective participation in group settings enhances one's ability to communicate with clarity and conviction. The capacity to articulate ideas, listen actively, and engage constructively is vital. These skills not only elevate the quality of group interactions but also nurture personal confidence and credibility. Individuals who frequently participate in varied group discussions tend to develop the keen ability to read the room, sensing not just the overt exchanges but the underlying emotional currents as well.

Furthermore, actively engaging in group interactions offers an unparalleled opportunity for learning. Each group presents a unique ecosystem of knowledge, perspectives, and experiences. As members share and debate ideas, they are exposed to viewpoints that challenge their preconceived notions and broaden their horizons. Over time, this exposure helps refine critical thinking skills and fosters an open-minded approach to problem-solving. By actively seeking out and valuing diverse perspectives, individuals can enrich their cognitive toolkit, sharpening their ability to innovate and adapt in an ever-changing environment.

Collaboration in groups is inherently intertwined with leadership development. By participating in diverse group settings, individuals naturally encounter scenarios that call for leadership qualities such as decisiveness, empathy, and vision. These environments serve as fertile ground for observing and experimenting with different leadership styles, allowing individuals to refine their approach and emerge as effective leaders themselves. This experiential learning is crucial, as it shapes one's ability to lead with authenticity and resilience, skills that are indispensable in both personal and professional arenas.

Engagement with group dynamics also provides fertile ground for emotional intelligence growth. Navigating the complexities of group behavior demands an acute awareness of one's emotions and those of others. Developing this emotional acuity enhances interpersonal relationships and creates a more profound empathy, critical for anyone looking to lead or collaborate successfully. Individuals often discover that as their emotional intelligence grows, so does their influence and acceptance within groups, opening doors to new opportunities and networks.

Moreover, frequent involvement in group interactions assists in honing adaptability, a trait that is increasingly essential in today's fast-paced world. Groups are dynamic entities, often subject to change in direction, membership, and objectives. The ability to adapt to these shifts gracefully is an invaluable skill. It involves being comfortable with ambiguity, managing unexpected outcomes, and embracing change as a constant. Cultivating adaptability can lead to more effective and less stressful navigation through both familiar and new situations.

A strategic focus on group dynamics can also empower one to build confidence in self-expression. The inherent support systems within groups can encourage individuals to voice their ideas and stand by their convictions. This is a cornerstone of professional development, translating to greater assertiveness in solo endeavors as well. The experience and feedback gained in group settings can affirm personal strengths and reveal areas for improvement, fostering an iterative process of self-assessment and enhancement.

Not to be underestimated, another personal benefit is the nurturing of patience and perseverance. Group interactions often require time and sustained effort to achieve desired results, teaching an approach to patience that is constructive rather than passive. This slow and steady commitment to a group goal can mirror the pursuit of long-term personal and professional goals. Understanding that success often emerges from persistence and resilience is a lesson that deeply impacts individual growth trajectories.

Finally, the strategic mastery of group dynamics can significantly expand one's professional network. Each group interaction creates connections across different arenas. These networks are invaluable for sharing resources, uncovering opportunities, and forging alliances. Professionals who cultivate diverse networks often find themselves at the intersection of innovation and opportunity, where they can leverage relationships to achieve personal and group goals more effectively.

To sum up, the strategies for personal and professional growth within the realm of group interactions are plentiful and varied. By delving into group dynamics, individuals sharpen their communication skills, learn adaptability, and nurture emotional intelligence. Beyond personal benefit, these strategies enhance group performance and success. The mutual development of personal growth and group accomplishment exemplifies how mastering group interactions becomes a transformative journey, leading to a fulfilling personal and professional life.

Long-Term Benefits of Mastering Group Dynamics

Understanding and harnessing the principles of group dynamics can have profound and lasting impacts, both personally and professionally. For anyone keen to delve into the world of group interactions, becoming adept at managing group dynamics unlocks a multitude of long-term benefits. At its core, mastering group dynamics helps individuals and teams communicate more effectively, make better decisions, and cultivate a more harmonious working environment. These improvements aren't just short-lived; they become ingrained in the way teams function and grow over time.

Consider enhanced communication, one of the most significant long-term benefits of understanding group dynamics. Effective communication within groups is crucial, and recognizing the nuances of how information flows among members can transform group interactions. This doesn't merely translate to getting ideas across with ease. Over time, it fosters an environment where members feel comfortable expressing their thoughts, leading to more innovative ideas, increased trust, and a clear alignment of goals—critical elements for any successful group endeavor.

Beyond communication, mastering group dynamics also impacts decision-making. When members feel their opinions are valued and understand how to work collaboratively, decisions are reached that are more inclusive and comprehensive. Over time, this results in better outcomes that reflect diverse perspectives and mitigate the risks of poor decision-making, often a pitfall of groupthink. The ability to make informed decisions collectively is an invaluable asset in any setting, whether it's navigating corporate landscapes or community planning.

Group dynamics mastery encourages personal growth as well. As individuals learn to interact and collaborate in group settings effectively, they develop essential skills such as empathy, patience, and resilience. These traits are not only beneficial in group contexts but also enhance personal relationships and individual well-being. Being attuned to the needs and motivations of others fosters a deeper understanding of oneself and promotes a more insightful approach to personal development. Long-term, these skills pave the way for personal and professional growth, allowing individuals to thrive in diverse environments.

Furthermore, understanding group dynamics strengthens leadership capabilities. Knowing how to harness the collective energy of a group towards a common goal is a hallmark of effective leadership.

Leaders who master group dynamics can inspire teams, drive change, and navigate challenges with agility. In the long run, this not only fortifies individual leadership skills but also contributes to building sustainable and adaptive group structures capable of weathering the ever-changing tides of business and social dynamics.

In teams where group dynamics are well-understood, one often observes a deeply ingrained culture of trust. Trust serves as the bedrock for any effective group. Over time, it raises morale, reduces conflict, and fosters an environment where members are eager to contribute and collaborate openly. The benefits of such trust extend beyond immediate interactions. Members take these experiences with them into future group settings, perpetuating a cycle of positive group-oriented behavior wherever they go.

The long-term advantages also touch upon conflict resolution skills. By studying group dynamics, one becomes adept at identifying potential sources of conflict and employing strategies to address them before they escalate. In environments where conflicts are managed constructively, creativity and innovation thrive. Groups are then empowered to face challenges boldly, leveraging each member's strengths to propel the group forward.

Moreover, recognizing and embracing the diversity within groups stands out as one of the most rewarding aspects of mastering group dynamics. Diverse teams bring varied perspectives and experiences to the table, which can be a powerful driver of innovation and problem-solving. By understanding and celebrating these differences, groups learn to harness them to their advantage. Over time, this not only benefits the group itself but also has a ripple effect in promoting inclusivity and respect in wider society.

From a larger perspective, being skilled at group dynamics prepares individuals and teams for the future. In a world where collaboration often crosses physical and digital borders, understanding how groups function is crucial. These skills form a foundation for adapting to new technologies and evolving work environments, ensuring that individuals remain relevant and competitive. Mastering the complexities of group dynamics fosters a readiness for navigating the challenges and seizing the opportunities of tomorrow.

Finally, it's worth noting the socio-cultural benefits of mastering group dynamics. With globalization and technological advances blurring geographic boundaries, understanding the cultural influences on group behavior becomes indispensable. Over time, this cultural competence not only enriches group interactions but also enhances one's ability to work and live harmoniously in a global society. The long-lasting impact is a more connected and empathetic world, where individuals harness group dynamics for collective good.

In conclusion, the benefits of mastering group dynamics extend well beyond immediate improvements in communication or conflict management. They lay the groundwork for sustained personal growth, effective leadership, and cohesive, innovative teams capable of tackling future challenges head-on. With perseverance and commitment to understanding and applying these principles, the long-term rewards prove immensely gratifying, both for individuals and the groups they engage with.

Conclusion

As we draw the threads of this exploration into group dynamics and behavior, it becomes evident that the fabric of group interaction is woven with complexity, diversity, and potential. Across the chapters, we've delved into the psychological intricacies that define how individuals come together to form cohesive units, whether these are teams, communities, or larger societal groups. The knowledge and strategies shared throughout this work aim to illuminate paths through which collective behavior can be effectively harnessed. In doing so, we aspire to provide you with insights not only into the underpinning mechanisms of group interactions but also into practical applications to enhance and elevate teamwork and leadership.

The journey through understanding group dynamics begins with recognizing the inherent nature of groups. They are more than just a collection of individuals; they are living systems where members influence and are influenced by each other. This interplay creates a synergy that, when nurtured properly, can propel groups toward remarkable achievements. In Chapter 1, we examined these foundational aspects, setting the stage for a deeper dive into the psychology of how groups shape behavior, and why social identity is integral to this process.

The chapters on decision-making and leadership emphasized that group outcomes are heavily influenced by these two pivotal factors. The dynamic between decision-making processes and leadership styles can foster an environment ripe for innovation or, conversely, one that stifles creativity and growth. Thus, embracing diverse perspectives, encouraging open communication, and promoting ethical leadership practices have the potential to significantly enhance group performance.

Communication and trust are the bedrock upon which effective group interaction is built. Without these, teams may struggle to find cohesion or resolve conflicts—common themes explored in Chapters 5 through 7. We underscored the importance of creating transparent communication channels, cultivating trust, and employing strategies to manage and resolve disputes. These are not just strategies for corporate settings but are universally applicable wherever teamwork is employed.

As diversity increasingly defines modern teams, Chapter 8 explored how diversity can be an engine for creativity and innovation, imparting teams with richer perspectives that fuel problem-solving and adaptability. However, embracing diversity requires intentionality in overcoming biases and fostering inclusive environments.

We also delved into motivation, emotions, and their profound impacts on group performance. Understanding what drives members, as detailed in Chapter 9, is crucial to optimizing productivity and satisfaction within the group. Additionally, acknowledging the role of emotions, as per Chapter 10, and employing emotional regulation techniques can help teams navigate the complexities of interpersonal dynamics more effectively.

Throughout the journey, the effects of technology on group interactions could not be understated. The landscape of collaboration is rapidly evolving, with remote teams and digital tools becoming commonplace. As highlighted in Chapter 12, while these advancements offer convenience, they also present unique challenges that require adaptation and strategic implementation of best practices.

Looking forward, as we examined in later chapters, the continuous evolution of group dynamics poses both challenges and opportunities. The future will demand that leaders and team members alike be agile, open to change, and equipped to navigate the technological, cultural, and ethical landscapes that define modern collaborative efforts.

At the heart of these discussions is the critical understanding that group success is not incidental. It is the culmination of insightful leadership, informed decision-making, adept communication, and an unwavering commitment to ethical principles. The case studies and real-world applications explored herein provide a roadmap for achieving these ends, showing how theory translates into practice effectively.

In the final analysis, mastering the power of group interactions is a transformative endeavor. It enriches personal and professional growth, offering long-term benefits that cascade beyond the confines of a single team or organization into broader societal progress. By integrating these insights and strategies into everyday group contexts, whether they're personal or professional, one can unlock the potential for extraordinary achievements.

Our conclusion, then, is a call to action. A call for leaders, team members, and individuals to apply the principles scattered throughout the chapters of this book, taking steps toward creating environments where everyone can thrive. The tapestry of group interaction is complex and delicate, yet immensely rewarding when approached with the right mindset and tools.

In closing, the power wielded by effective groups is transformational. It influences not only immediate tasks and objectives but fundamentally shapes the culture and trajectory of companies and societies. Embrace this opportunity to harness the collective energies of your teams and communities, drive innovations, and forge paths of progress that lead to a more collaborative, understanding, and impactful future.

Appendix A:
Appendix

As we cross the finish line of our exploration into the intricate world of group dynamics, this appendix serves as a compass pointing toward further reflection and application. Throughout the chapters, we've delved deep into the mechanisms that govern the behavior of groups, unraveling the tapestry of interactions that drive collective achievements and challenges.

This section is crafted to amplify your understanding and provide ready-to-hand resources for putting theory into practice. It includes selected references and additional reading materials vital to anyone eager to comprehend and influence group behavior more effectively. Here, we also hope to encapsulate key concepts and frameworks that underline successful teamwork and leadership, providing a quick reference guide to reinforce your learning.

Each topic within the main body of this work has been meticulously chosen to illustrate the multifaceted nature of human collaboration. From leadership styles and decision-making processes to the emotional and cultural factors that subtly shape group behavior, this appendix frames and reflects on each element, inviting you to integrate these insights into your own contexts.

Moreover, consider this appendix not just as an ending, but a potential launch pad for future discoveries. With the global landscape of work continually evolving, understanding group dynamics propels us toward new realms of creativity, efficiency, and innovation. As business leaders, team managers, social scientists, or simply curious individuals, your journey into mastering group interactions doesn't conclude here; it expands with every new experience and challenge.

In essence, view this section as your toolkit—a collection of strategies and principles capable of transforming mere groups into cohesive units working seamlessly toward shared goals. As we continue to navigate the complexities of human behavior, may this appendix remain a trusted guide, steadying your steps on the path to effective collaboration.

Thank you for joining this exploration. Here's to the power of groups and the potential within each of us to harness it.

www.ingramcontent.com/pod-product-compliance
Lightning Source LLC
Chambersburg PA
CBHW022250290526
45785CB00015B/499